# Discourse and Practice

# OXFORD STUDIES IN SOCIOLINGUISTICS

General Editors:

Nikolas Coupland
Adam Jaworski
*Cardiff University*

Recently Published in the Series:

*Talking about Treatment: Recommendations for Breast Cancer Adjuvant Treatment*
Felicia D. Roberts

*Language in Time: The Rhythm and Tempo of Spoken Interaction*
Peter Auer, Elizabeth Kuhlen, Frank Müller

*Whales, Candlelight, and Stuff Like That: General Extenders in English Discourse*
Maryann Overstreet

*A Place to Stand: Politics and Persuasion in a Working-Class Bar*
Julie Lindquist

*Sociolinguistics Variation: Critical Reflections*
Edited by Carmen Fought

*Prescribing under Pressure: Parent-Physician Conversations and Antibiotics*
Tanya Stivers

*Discourse and Practice: New Tools for Critical Discourse Analysis*
Theo van Leeuwen

# Discourse and Practice

## *New Tools for Critical Discourse Analysis*

Theo van Leeuwen

OXFORD
UNIVERSITY PRESS

2008

# OXFORD
UNIVERSITY PRESS

Oxford University Press, Inc., publishes works that further
Oxford University's objective of excellence
in research, scholarship, and education.

Oxford   New York
Auckland   Cape Town   Dar es Salaam   Hong Kong   Karachi
Kuala Lumpur   Madrid   Melbourne   Mexico City   Nairobi
New Delhi   Shanghai   Taipei   Toronto

With offices in
Argentina   Austria   Brazil   Chile   Czech Republic   France   Greece
Guatemala   Hungary   Italy   Japan   Poland   Portugal   Singapore
South Korea   Switzerland   Thailand   Turkey   Ukraine   Vietnam

Published by Oxford University Press, Inc.
198 Madison Avenue, New York, New York 10016

www.oup.com

Oxford is a registered trademark of Oxford University Press

Library of Congress Cataloging-in-Publication Data
Leeuwen, Theo van.
Discourse and practice : new tools for critical discourse analysis / Theo van Leeuwen.
   p. cm.—(Oxford studies in sociolinguistics)
ISBN  978-0-19-532330-6; 978-0-19-532331-3 (pbk.)
1. Critical discourse analysis.   I. Title.
P302.L433 2008
401'.41—dc22          2007023090

Printed in the United States of America
on acid-free paper

To Jesse,
who has just experienced
his first day at school

# PREFACE

This book brings together most of my work on critical discourse analysis of the past 15 years, focusing on the theoretical and methodological papers and drawing occasionally on the more "applied" papers for additional examples. In this work I developed an analytical framework for discourse analysis which derives, on the one hand, from Michel Foucault's concept of discourses as semantic constructions of specific aspects of reality that serve the interests of particular historical and/or social contexts, and, on the other hand, from Michael Halliday's concept of "register" as a semantic variety of language, a social dialect which is distinct in its semantics rather than in its phonology and lexicogrammar.

The approach behind my framework is Bernstein's concept of recontextualization. In the move from the context in which knowledge is produced to the pedagogic context in which it is reproduced and disseminated, Bernstein argued, semantic shifts take place "according to recontextualizing principles which selectively appropriate, relocate, refocus and relate to other discourses to constitute its own order and orderings" (Bernstein, 1990: 184). My work broadens this concept beyond pedagogic discourse and starts from the assumption that all discourses recontextualize social practices, and that all knowledge is, therefore, ultimately grounded in practice, however slender that link may seem at times.

The recontextualizing principles that are the subject of this book are therefore linked to key elements of social practices: actors and their roles and identities, actions and their performance styles, settings, and timings. In the process of recontextualization, aspects of any of these may be excluded from the discourse or transformed, and recontextualization may also add elements such as purposes and legitimations for the actions. As a result, some recontextualizations eliminate much of the actual detail of the social practices they recontextualize and focus, for instance, mostly on legitimation or critique, while others focus on the social practices themselves and contain few elements of legitimation or critique. This book provides a detailed account of these recontextualizing principles, describing how, for instance, social actors, or the timing of social practices, *can* be recontextualized and exemplifying how they are in fact recontextualized in specific discursive contexts.

Discourses, as I conceive of them in this book, can be realized, not only linguistically, but also by means of other semiotic modes. In the final chapter, the two main areas in which I have worked, critical discourse analysis and multimodal semiotics, come together when I show how social actors can be recontextualized visually and in children's play, through Playmobil, a children's toy "system" specifically designed as a resource for representing the social world in play.

Six of the book's nine chapters have been previously published more or less in the form in which they are included here, though I have removed repetitive material and integrated the chapters as best as possible. The introductory chapter, the chapter on the recontextualization of space, and the final chapter have not been published before.

Chapter 1 builds upon my article "Genre and Field in Critical Discourse Analysis: A Synopsis," in *Discourse and Society* 4(2):193–225 (1993), and "Language and Representation: The Recontextualisation of Participants, Activities and Reactions," my Ph.D. thesis, University of Sydney, chapters 1, 2, and 3.

Chapter 2 is a slightly changed version of my essay "The Representation of Social Actors," in C. R. Caldas-Coulthard and M. Coulthard (Eds.), *Texts and Practices: Readings in Critical Discourse Analysis* (London: Routledge, 1996), pp. 32–70; used by permission of Thomson Publishing Services.

Chapter 3 is a slightly changed version of my article "Representing Social Action," in *Discourse and Society* 6(1):81–106 (1995); used by permission of Sage Publications.

Chapter 4 is a reworked version of my article "Time in Discourse," *Linguistics and the Human Sciences* 1(1):125–45 (2005); used by permission of Equinox Publishing, Ltd.

An earlier version of chapter 6 appeared as Van Leeuwen (2007), "Legitimation in Discourse and Communication," in *Discourse and Communication* 1(1):91–112; used by permission of Sage Publications.

Chapter 7 is a slightly altered version of Van Leeuwen (2000a), "The Construction of Purpose in Discourse," in S. Sarangi and M. Coulthard (Eds.), *Discourse and Social Life* (London: Longman), pp. 66–82; used by permission of Pearson Education Ltd.

Chapter 8 is a revised version of Van Leeuwen (2000b), "Visual Racism." In M. Reisigl and R. Wodak (Eds.), *The Semiotics of Racism: Approaches in Critical Discourse Analysis* (Vienna: Passagen Verlag), pp. 330–50; used by permission of Passagen Verlag.

The research for chapter 9 was part of the research program Toys as Communication led by Professor Staffan Selander of the Institute of Education, Stockholm, and financed by a grant from the Swedish Royal Bank. Videos of children playing with Playmobil in a Birmingham preschool and in their home settings were recorded by Dr. Carmen Caldas-Coulthard.

I would like to thank Jim Martin, who supervised the Ph.D. thesis in which I began this work and whose work on activity sequences was a key inspiration, and Michael Halliday, without whose help with grammar the work could not have been done. Norman Fairclough, Teun van Dijk, Ruth Wodak, and Gunther Kress, the original "critical discourse analysis group," were supportive colleagues and friends throughout the years in which I did this work. Thanks also to Nik Coupland and Adam Jaworski, colleagues and friends from my Cardiff years, who helped to conceive of this book in its early stages and agreed to include it in their series, and to Roz Ivanic, who, perhaps more than anyone else, used my ideas in her teaching and fed back to me her own comments and those of her students.

# CONTENTS

# Discourse and Practice

# Discourse as the Recontextualization of Social Practice

In this chapter, I discuss the central idea of this book, its conception of discourse as recontextualized social practice. I then introduce the elements of social practices and their recontextualizations. In subsequent chapters, I deal with most of these elements in greater depth.

## 1. The Supersedure of Meaning by Function

Max Weber (1977) described "rationalization" as a form of social organization in which social action is no longer oriented toward meanings, values, and beliefs, but toward strategies, no longer toward the questions "Is it true?" "Is it good?" but toward the questions "Does it work?" "Does it achieve its purposes?" As a result, rationalized social action is proceduralized, turned into a step-by-step method through intricate legalistic rules that aim at achieving the purpose of the action more efficiently and economically. In rationalized social interaction, it is therefore no longer consensual representation which binds the members of society together, but common practice, procedures. Meaning loses its bearings and becomes fragmented and heterogeneous. Social action becomes increasingly regimented, homogenized, and proceduralized. This is what Zijderveld (1979) called the "supersedure of meaning by function in modernity."

It is not difficult to think of examples. In universities, a plurality of discourses is permitted. Marxist philosophy can be taught side by side with total quality management and social biology. No unifying doctrine or belief is needed to guarantee the cohesion of the institution. But there are increasingly many rules to specify *how* all of these subjects should be taught, and these are increasingly "one size fits all" rules that do not respect the differences between different subjects and that must be adhered to in the same way by architects and astrologers, nurses and nuclear physicists. In other spheres of social life, it is no different. Global media, for instance, allow content to be diverse and localized, but homogenize formats and genres to an unprecedented degree (Machin and Van Leeuwen, 2003, 2004). Everywhere, there are fewer (and more powerful) procedures and formats and templates, and more (but less powerful) discourses. Everywhere, there is generic homogeneity and discursive heterogeneity.

At the same time as the rise of managerialism and the market culture gave new impetus to these developments in the 1970s, linguists were developing theories of genre to analyze texts in terms of content-free, strategically motivated procedures. Labov (1972) still thought he was writing about the boasting stories of Harlem teenagers, but the content-free categories of his narrative schema have since been applied successfully to many other types of story, written as well as spoken, factual as well as fictional. In the early '80s, Martin defined genre as a "linguistically realised activity type" (1984a: 3) and a "goal-oriented social process" (1984b: 32). Other genre theories of the 1980s and '90s followed the same line. Given the increasing proceduralization of social action, it is clearly important that genre should be studied in this way. But then it was not done critically; on the contrary, with very few exceptions (e.g., Kress and Threadgold, 1988), genres were viewed as powerful and hence empowering discourse "technologies," rather than critiqued as examples of what Foucault has called the "microphysics of power" (e.g., 1978: 59ff.). And it was also done at the expense of representation. From the point of view of critical discourse analysis, texts should be studied as representations as well as interactions (strategic or otherwise). It is for this reason that I seek to turn things around in this book and work with a corpus of texts that vary in terms of genre but are united in terms of what they represent.

## 2. Discourse as the Recontextualization of Social Practice

Anthropologists and sociologists have always realized that representation is ultimately based on practice, on "what people do." The primacy of practice runs like a thread through European and American sociology. It is true that sociologists sometimes derive concrete actions from abstract concepts, and processes from systems—Durkheim's "collective consciousness," Bourdieu's "habitus," Talcott Parsons' systems theory (1977), and Lévi-Strauss's structuralist anthropology are examples. Yet the primacy of practice keeps asserting itself also in the work of these writers, sometimes against the grain of their general methodology. Bourdieu elaborated the primacy of practice and the fundamental difference between participant knowledge and "outsider" knowledge in *Outline of a Theory of Practice* (1977) and elsewhere. Talcott Parsons, even in his systems theory, can still say that "the subject of social interaction is in a fundamental sense logically prior to that of social system" (1977: 145). Even Lévi-Strauss (1964) at times derives the meaning of myths from social practices rather than from abstract schemata. And Durkheim, especially in *The Elementary Forms of Religious Life* (1976) and *Primitive Classification* (Durkheim and Mauss,

1963), leaves no doubt about it: myths are modeled after rites, conceptual life after social life, representations of the world after social organization:

> The first logical categories were social categories.... It was because men were grouped, and thought of themselves in the form of groups, that in their ideas they grasped other things, and in the beginning the two modes of groupings were merged to the point of being indistinct. Moieties were the first genera, clans the first species. Things were thought to be integral parts of society, and it was their place in society which determined their place in nature. (Durkheim and Mauss, 1963: 82–83)

In linguistics, things have generally been the other way around, with systems (grammars, paradigms) generating processes (syntagms), rather than processes (practices) generating systems (institutions and objectified forms of knowledge). But when linguists began to study texts, in the 1970s, many found it hard to conceptualize the production and interpretation of texts without recourse to experience, to "world knowledge" (e.g., Schank and Abelson, 1977), or "background knowledge" (e.g., Levinson, 1983; Brown and Yule, 1987), etc. Martin (1984a, 1988, 1989), at the same time as developing his genre theory, reintroduced the "field" of discourse, using lexical cohesion analysis to construct "activity sequences"—sequences of *represented* activities, this time, rather than the sequences of communicative activities that constitute genres. Together with the work of Gleason (1973) and Grimes (1977), who paid attention, not just to represented activities, but also to represented "roles," "settings," etc., this work has been a fundamental influence on the ideas presented in this book. But Martin's examples are procedural texts, in which there is considerable congruity between the order of the text as an activity and the order of the activities it represents. The same can be said about the narrative texts in Grimes. I will take the view that all texts, all representations of the world and what is going on in it, however abstract, should be interpreted as representations of social practices. In analyzing expository or argumentative texts, I will not replace "activity sequences" with concepts such as "thematic structures" (Lemke, 1983, 1985) or "implication sequences" (Martin et al., 1988). Instead, I will analyze all texts for the way they draw on, and transform, social practices. It may be argued that in some cases this cannot be done. What about weather reports, for instance? Surely the weather is not a social practice? No, but whenever reference is made to it in texts, it will be, and can only be, via social practices or elements thereof. Weather reports, for instance, objectivate the social practices of meteorologists— practices of observation, of recording, and of performing mathematical and linguistic operations on these observations and recordings. As Malinowski has said:

> Even in the most abstract and theoretical aspects of human thought and verbal usage, the real understanding of words ultimately derives from active experience of those aspects of reality to which the words belong. The chemist or physicist understands his most abstract concepts ultimately on the basis of his acquaintance with chemical and physical processes in the laboratory. Even the pure mathematician, dealing with that most useless and arrogant branch of his learning, the theory of numbers, has probably had some experience of counting his pennies and shillings or his boots and buns. In short, there is no science whose conceptual, hence verbal, outfit is not ultimately derived from the practical handling of matter. (Malinowski, 1935: 58)

It is important to stress the difference between social practices and representations of social practices. It seems obvious, yet the difference is often glossed over. Martin (1984b: 5), in discussing a text about dog showing, does not draw a line between activity types which do and activity types which do not represent other activities or activity types: "Feeding is just as much part of dog showing whether one is doing it or talking about it." Again, for Schank and Abelson (1977), the same "scripts" underlie our ability to participate in social practices and our ability to represent them. Here I will insist on the difference between "doing it" and "talking about it," and on the plurality of discourses—the many different possible ways that the same social practice can be represented. To do so, I will use Bernstein's concept of "recontextualization" (1981, 1986). Bernstein introduced this concept in relation to educational practices. He described how knowledge is actively *produced* in "the upper reaches of the education system" (1986: 5) and then embedded into a pedagogic content in the "lower reaches" where it is objectified and made to serve the contextually defined purpose of a "discourse of order," that is, of "moral education" in the Durkheimian sense. Here I will use Bernstein's concept in a more general sense and connect it to the term "discourse," which I use here in Foucault's sense (e.g., 1977), that is, not in the sense of "an extended stretch of connected speech or writing," a "text," but in the sense of social cognition, of "a socially constructed knowledge of some social practice," developed in specific social contexts, and in ways appropriate to these contexts, whether these contexts are large, for instance multinational corporations, or small, for instance particular families, and whether they are strongly institutionalized, for instance the press, or less so, for instance dinner table conversations.

As discourses are social cognitions, socially specific ways of knowing social practices, they can be, and are, used as resources for representing social practices in text. This means that it is possible to reconstruct discourses from the texts that draw on them. This book is for the most part based on a corpus of texts dealing with "the first day of school," a key rite of passage in modern life. It includes a wide range of text types—books for very young children, brochures for parents, media reports, advertisements for school gear, teacher training texts, reminiscences in short stories and novels, texts that are critical of schooling such as Ivan Illich's *Deschooling Society* (1973), and more. In other words, the corpus is generically diverse, but at the same time united in that all these texts represent the same social practice, or some aspect of it. In doing so, they do not of course confine themselves to representing only the activities of "the first day," their settings, and so on. In Foucault's words (1977: 135), discourses not only involve "a field of objects," but also "the definition of a legitimate perspective for the agent of knowledge" in a given context (ibid.). They not only represent what is going on, they also evaluate it, ascribe purposes to it, justify it, and so on, and in many texts these aspects of representation become far more important than the representation of the social practice itself.

## 3. Social Practices

Social practices are socially regulated ways of doing things—but the word "regulate" may give the wrong impression here, since "regulation," in the sense in which we normally understand it, is only one of the ways in which social coordination can be achieved. Different social practices are "regulated" to different degrees and in different ways—for instance, through strict prescription, or through traditions, or through the influence of experts and charismatic role models, or through the constraints of technological resources used, and so on (cf. Van Leeuwen, 2005a: ch. 3).

In this section, I present the model of social practice I will use in this book, using one specific text to show how elements of social practices enter into texts. The example is a short newspaper article from the "family pages" of the *Daily Mirror*, a Sydney, Australia, tabloid newspaper, which appeared a few days before the beginning of the school year:

> 1.1 "When Mum first took me to school I started to cry because I thought I would never see her again."
>
> "But after a few days I really loved school."—Mark, aged six.
>
> Mark, now 10, quickly discovered starting school wasn't as "scary" as he thought.
>
> Mark was one of the many children teacher-turned-author Valerie Martin spoke to when writing From Home to School, a book dealing with the first day.
>
> "The first day at school can be a happy and memorable one," Valerie said.
>
> "But the secret is getting ready and preparing now."
>
> Valerie said the main problems for new pupils were separation from families, meeting large numbers of children they didn't know and conforming to a classroom situation.
>
> Here are some of Valerie's suggestions to help take the hassle out of the big day. Over the next few days try to get your child used to:
>
> - putting on and taking off clothes
> - tying shoe laces
> - eating and drinking without help
> - using a handkerchief
>
> Valerie says it is important your child knows how to:
>
> - use and flush a toilet
> - ask for things clearly
> - say his or her name and address
> - cross a road safely
>
> On the first day it is important not to rush children. Valerie says give them plenty of time to get ready, eat breakfast and wash and clean their teeth.
>
> If possible, get everything ready the night before because children become unsettled if they have to rush.
>
> "And finally don't worry if you or your child cries," Valerie says. "It won't last long."

Although not all are always represented, I assume here that all actually performed social practices include all of the following elements:

## (1) Participants

A social practice first of all needs a set of participants in certain roles (principally those of instigator, agent, affected, or beneficiary). A lecture minimally needs a lecturer and students. "Going to school for the first time" minimally needs parents, children, and teachers, and other school staff might also be involved. Example 1.1 above intertwines reference to four social practices, each with its own set of participants:

(a) *Mothers* hand over their *children* to a *teacher* on "the big day."
(b) An *expert author*, through the medium of a book, counsels *mothers* on how to prepare their *children* for the first day.
(c) The *expert author* interviews *children* as part of her research for a book on the first day.
(d) *Mothers* prepare their *children* for the first day.

Not all of the participants are explicitly mentioned in the text. There is no mention of the teacher, for instance. Clearly, recontextualizations can exclude some of the participants of the practices they recontextualize. This will be discussed in more detail below.

Example 1.1 can itself also be viewed as a social practice:

(e) A *journalist* reports to *readers* of the "family pages" the counsel of an expert author and, in this way, indirectly counsels those of her readers who are also parents.

But the key participants (journalist and readers) are not realized in and by the text, nor are the many other participants involved in the production and distribution of newspapers. The text only realizes the journalist's *actions* (reporting). The other elements of the practice are usually seen as "context." But as the concept of "social practice" combines both "text" and "context," the latter concept becomes perhaps somewhat redundant here.

## (2) Actions

The core of any social practice is a set of actions performed in a sequence, which may be fixed to a greater or lesser degree and which may or may not allow for choice, that is, for alternatives with regard to a greater or lesser number of the actions of some or all of the participants, and for concurrence, that is, for the simultaneity of different actions during part or all of the sequence. The following actions belonging to the social practice of the first day are represented in example 1.1—though not in the order in which they would actually have to be performed:

1. Mother takes child to school.
2. Teacher separates child from mother.
3. Child starts to cry.
4. Child meets large number of children.
5. Child conforms to classroom situation.
6. Child discovers school is not "scary."
7. Child loves school.

I will discuss later why the actual order of the actions is changed in the text. Here the point is that it is to some extent possible to reconstruct the order in which the represented actions must have actually taken place. Actions 1 and 2, for instance, must have clearly occurred in the sequence listed above, as do the child's reactions (actions 3, 5, and 7). But about actions 2, 4 and 6 we cannot be so sure. Literature on managing the first day (e.g., Cleave et al., 1982, ch. 8) shows that in some schools children can meet the other children before, in others only after they are separated from the mother. The practice of "going to school for the first time" is not so closely regulated that the sequence of events is entirely determined.

The second social practice represented in 1.1 is "preparing children for the first day." The following actions are listed:

1. Mother teaches child to put on and take off clothes.
2. Mother teaches child to tie shoelaces.
3. Mother teaches child to eat and drink without help.
4. Mother teaches child to use a handkerchief.
5. Mother teaches child to use and flush a toilet.
6. Mother teaches child to ask for things clearly.
7. Mother teaches child to say his or her name and address.
8. Mother teaches child to cross a road safely.

These actions are in fact names for smaller-scale action *sequences*, and if "Valerie's suggestions" had been more than suggestions and included precise instructions on how to teach a child to eat and drink, blow her nose, etc., it would have been possible to describe them as linear sequences. As they are represented here, it does not seem possible to reconstruct any order in which they would necessarily have to have occurred. Perhaps this shows that the social practices of the family are not as proceduralized, not as precisely sequenced as the social practices of school life. Different social practices involve different degrees of freedom, different margins for resistance—and different modes of enforcing conformity: a mother who does not teach her child to blow her nose may be considered slightly negligent; a mother who does not take her child to school will get in trouble with the law.

The social practice of "counseling parents for the first day," as represented in 1.1, includes the following actions:

1. The expert author asserts that the first day can be happy and memorable.
2. The expert author warns that this is so only on the condition that parents prepare their children properly.
3. The expert author states the problem.
4. The expert author suggests the solutions.
5. The expert author counsels not to rush children.
6. The expert author counsels not to worry and predicts success.

These actions of course are speech acts, and the practice of giving counsel is therefore a practice which recontextualizes another practice. Here, too, we can reconstruct the order in which the actions would have to be performed—but not with certainty.

Actions 3 and 4, for instance, must necessarily appear in the order shown above, but actions 1 and 2 might have followed 6, as a kind of summary. Here, too, different social contexts offer writers and speakers different amounts of freedom. And the rules, or strategies, or best practice models they follow are not autonomous linguistic structure potentials, but modalities of institutionalized social control that should themselves be studied as different kinds of practices.

### (3) Performance Modes

In our example text, parents are advised "not to rush children." When "preparing children for the first day," it is apparently not enough to perform the actions that make up the practice, they must also be performed at a certain pace, and the need to be unhurried does not relate to all of the actions but only to those that are performed "the night before" and "on the first day" itself.

Representations of social practices are full of such "stage directions," or *performance modes*, as I will call them here.

### (4) Eligibility Conditions (Participants)

*Eligibility conditions* are the "qualifications" participants must have in order to be eligible to play a particular role in a particular social practice.

In example 1.1, for instance, Mark is "aged six": to be eligible for the role of child in the social practice of the first day, a certain age is required. Similarly, to be eligible for the role of "expert author," certain "qualifications" are necessary: Valerie is represented as having experience as a teacher (she is a "teacher-turned-author") and as having researched her topic with thorough, quantitative methods (she has "spoken to many children").

Such eligibility conditions refer to further social practices: the social practice (by no means universal) of keeping track of people's ages by means of a certain calendar, in the one case, and the social practices of teaching and social science research, in the other. The relation of "preparatory practice" to "core practice" is just one of the ways in which social practices can be interconnected—and a practice which, in one context, is "preparatory" may be "core" in another.

### (5) Presentation Styles

Social practices also involve dress and body grooming requirements, or *presentation styles*, for the participants.

In 1.1, these are stated mainly in terms of hygiene. The child should be clean and have brushed her teeth. The advertisements which appeared in the same issue of the same newspaper were more explicit and showed the clothes that children should wear to school: "they'll start the new term in fine style with the top brands from Grace Bros! Fine quality, super value and vast choice of regulation gear!"

Presentation styles may be explicitly prescribed (school and other uniforms, wedding rings, and so on) or not, and social practices vary a great deal in the amount of freedom they leave to (some or all of) the participants in this respect. But dress and body grooming requirements are never entirely absent. Even people who work at home alone, unobserved by anyone, will dress for the activities of the day in socially regulated ways. Like performance modes, presentation styles may apply to the whole of a social practice or to specific parts of it: the wearing and taking off of hats by men during certain social practices (e.g., burials) is one example. And like eligibility conditions, presentation styles connect to preparatory practices, such as dressing, shaving, hair dressing, makeup, and so on.

## (6) Times

Social practices and specific parts of them take place at more or less definite times.

In the example text, several time constraints are indicated: the social practice of going to school for the first time must take place when the child has reached the age of six and on a specific day, the beginning of the school year. The child's adaptation to school life happens "quickly." "Getting everything ready" must occur "the night before." "Preparing children for the first day" takes place "over the next few days," i.e., during the days prior to the beginning of the school year.

The other social practices referred to in our example are not linked to specific (or unspecific) times, and would therefore seem to be free of time constraints. However, although the time constraints on social practices vary in strictness, they are never fully absent: the writing and publishing of books, for instance, are subject to time schedules, and counseling on how to "prepare" children for the first day must take place toward the time that such preparation is due to begin, i.e., in the run-up to starting school. It is just that in this case they have not been represented.

## (7) Locations

Social practices are also related to specific locations.

The two main locations in example 1.1 are "home" and "school." Other locations mentioned are "the toilet" and "the road." But on the whole, the text is not very explicit about location, and we will see later that in other texts about the same topic, e.g., texts written for children and for teachers of young children, location is referred to in considerably more detail.

Practices may involve changing from one location to another. The first day, for example, may involve not only the classroom, but also the playground, the hall, the cloakroom, and so on. Within the classroom, the furniture may be rearranged for the various activities that make up the first school day.

## (8) Eligibility Conditions (Locations)

Example 1.1 does not refer to conditions of this kind, but it is clear that rooms must fulfill certain conditions if they are to qualify as classrooms or living rooms or kitchens. Such conditions will relate to the size and shape of the room as well as to its decoration or lack thereof (e.g., whether the floor is covered with a carpet, or tiles, or linoleum; what colors are used for the floor and the walls) and, especially, to the furniture and the way it is arranged, at least in contemporary Western culture.

In other cultures, the distance between, and the postures of, the participants, rather than "fixed feature arrangements," might suffice to make a room into a classroom or living room.

Like the eligibility conditions for participants, the eligibility conditions for locations refer back to "preparatory practices"—of building, of interior decorating, of arranging furniture, of cleaning. And, different social institutions will allow a different amount of freedom with regard to each of the aspects mentioned.

(9)  Resources: Tools and Materials

Example 1.1 related "preparing your child for the first day" to several material resources—shoes (with laces) to teach children how to tie shoelaces, and handkerchiefs to teach them how to blow their noses.

The "props" needed to perform a practice or some part of it may again connect with other practices, for example, practices of time keeping: clocks are a crucial tool for strictly scheduled social practices, and so is the school bell in the case of schooling.

(10)  Eligibility Conditions (Resources)

Like participants and locations, tools and materials are subject to eligibility conditions: not any bag qualifies as a schoolbag; not any piece of paper qualifies as material for the activity of learning how to write. How much room for interpretation there is in these conditions will vary from practice to practice, but some conditions will always apply.

Table 1.1 summarizes this section by showing, in tabular form, how the elements discussed here relate to each other. In this table, and other similar tables in this books, the arrows connecting the activities will indicate a linear sequence. Where choice occurs, there will be bifurcating arrows, as in flow diagrams, and where it is not possible to assign sequence a ≈ sign will be used instead of the arrows. The example is based on part of a children's story (Leete-Hodge, n.d.).

## 4. The Recontextualization Chain

In recontextualization, the recontextualized social practice may be (1) a sequence of nonlinguistic actions, for example, dressing or having breakfast, (2) a sequence in which linguistic and nonlinguistic actions alternate ("language in action"; see Malinowski, 1923), or (3) a sequence of linguistic (and/or other semiotic) actions (a "genre," in the sense of, e.g., Martin, 1992). The *recontextualizing* social practice, however, must always be a sequence of linguistic (and/or other semiotic) activities, a "genre."

Recontextualization not only makes the recontextualized social practices explicit to a greater or lesser degree, it also makes them pass through the filter of the practices in which they are inserted. The way in which this happens is rarely transparent to the participants of the recontextualizing practice, and is usually embedded

TABLE 1.1. Social Practice Analysis of an Excerpt from *Mark and Mandy* (Leete-Hodge, n.d.)

| Actions | Participants | Eligibility Conditions | Presentation Styles | Times | Locations | Eligibility Conditions | Resources | Eligibility Conditions |
|---|---|---|---|---|---|---|---|---|
| set out ↓ | Mark, Mandy, their mothers; Mandy's baby sister, Debbie; Mark's dog, Smudge | Mark and Mandy are five years old | Mark: green shirt, dark trousers | "far too early" on "the great day" | Elm Street | | satchels | new |
| | | | Mandy: red dress, white blouse, red bow in hair | | | | | |
| arrive ↓ | | | | | school | tall, with a high fence and a big road sign | | |
| tell the dog to wait outside ↓ | Mark | | | | | | | |
| greet Mark and Mandy ↓ | Teacher | | smiling | | at the door | | | |
| invite Mark and Mandy ↓ | Teacher | | | | | | | |
| follow the teacher | Mark and Mandy | | | "before they knew it" | down a long corridor | | | |

in their common sense, in their habits of relating to each other, and in what they take the purposes of the recontextualizing practice to be—all those things which form the usually tacit know-how of experienced participants of the recontextualizing social practice.

Recontextualization is also recursive—it can happen over and over again, removing us further and further from the starting point of the chain of recontextualizations.

Table 1.2 reconstructs the history of example 1.1. It starts with the practice of "preparing your child for the first day," with the things that mothers actually do to ensure that their children are ready for school. To mothers, this would not appear to be an activity which follows a clear-cut recipe, but a new situation requiring specific strategies, even if they rely on what their mothers did ("times have changed") or have already gone through it with another child ("every child is different"). Were they asked precisely what they do and why they do it, they might find it difficult to know exactly what to say. Yet in doing it they may be influenced by discourses about the practice—for instance, by books such as Valerie Martin's, or by articles such as our example text, or perhaps by discussions with friends and relatives.

This initial practice is then inserted into another one, the practice of interviewing children for research purposes. In the process, it will be recontextualized: the assumptions, values, and goals pertinent to research on this subject will inform the interviewer's questions and also, even if perhaps with room for different views, the interviewees' answers.

The texts resulting from the interviews, in turn, are inserted into yet another practice, the practice of "counseling parents by means of a book." Another recontextualization takes place, in which, for example, the difference between differing views may be reduced, or even removed, and in which, as a result of the new goal of "counseling" and the new social relation between the "professional expert" and the "lay parent," "what parents and children do" (as ascertained by the interviews) is recontextualized to become "what parents and children *should* do."

The book, itself a recontextualization, is then inserted into the social practice of journalism, and, in the process, "preparing children for the first day" is recontextualized yet again. News reports, when making general statements about the world, attribute these to experts and other authorities—unattributed statements must relate to specific events with temporal proximity to the date of publication (here, "the first day"). This particular news report appeared in the "family" section of the paper and therefore could be said to have, next to the goal of "reporting," another goal, that of "providing a service to families": it not only reports what the expert has said, it also, though only obliquely, counsels readers who are also parents of young children.

The generic structure of the article provides some evidence of what the writer is trying to achieve with this recontextualization. I have discussed this aspect of this example in more detail elsewhere (Van Leeuwen, 1987a) and will here only give a brief summary.

The text contains four distinct generic stages and one speech act ("Mark was one of the many children teacher-turned-author Valerie Martin spoke to") which could either be seen as belonging to stage 1 or as belonging to stage 2. I will call it a "hinge." In other words, it begins as a mini-narrative, and then moves into an expository account of the first day as "problem." This is followed by a series of adhortations addressed to parents, and a prediction of good results if the expert's advice is followed. A conclusive conjunction links the adhortations to the exposition of the "problem." In short, the text first draws its readers in with a short confessional narrative, a story of individual experience with which they can identify easily. It then generalizes the story, turning it into a "problem" which is analyzed and interpreted in the authoritative language of the expert. A series of do's and don'ts for parents is

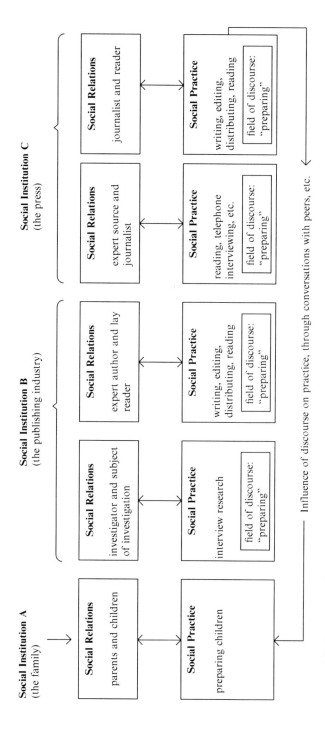

TABLE 1.2. Recontextualization Chain

**Social Institution A**
(the family)

**Social Institution B**
(the publishing industry)

**Social Institution C**
(the press)

| **Social Relations**<br>parents and children |
| **Social Practice**<br>preparing children |

| **Social Relations**<br>investigator and subject of investigation |
| **Social Practice**<br>interview research<br><br>field of discourse: "preparing" |

| **Social Relations**<br>expert author and lay reader |
| **Social Practice**<br>writing, editing, distributing, reading<br><br>field of discourse: "preparing" |

| **Social Relations**<br>expert source and journalist |
| **Social Practice**<br>reading, telephone interviewing, etc.<br><br>field of discourse: "preparing" |

| **Social Relations**<br>journalist and reader |
| **Social Practice**<br>writing, editing, distributing, reading<br><br>field of discourse: "preparing" |

—— Influence of discourse on practice, through conversations with peers, etc.

then distilled from this analysis, and finally success is predicted—always provided that the instructions are adhered to.

Confessional narrative
↓
Hinge
↓
Discussion: analysis of the general
problem distilled from the narrative
↓
Adhortation: solution of the problem
in the form of instructions
↓
Prediction of success (happy ending)

This structure realizes a particular kind of discursive practice, the kind of short, secular sermon common in advice columns on problems of health, beauty, child rearing, sexuality, etc. The following short text, from the agony column of an upmarket women's magazine, employs more or less the same structure, albeit within the context of a question (1–5) and answer (6–15) format:

1.2  (1) I am a 35-year-old mother who loves her husband very much (2) but I can't stop imagining every second man I see as a lover, be it men we both know, movie actors, or the guy from the petrol station. (3) When I'm making love to my husband it's much more exciting to imagine he's the neighbour or my husband's mate. (4) What is wrong with me? (5) Why can't I be content with one partner happily ever after?

(6) Mid-30s and over are often a sexually restless time for women. (7) At this age a lot of women, like you, have been with the same man for many years. (8) Many are just coming out of that sexually dampening period of caring for young children (9) and are beginning to relax and enjoy their sexuality in a way that was not possible earlier in their lives. (10) In such circumstances, the desire is very natural. (11) Sexual curiosity tends to take over, leaving us wondering and fantasising in a way we never did before. (12) So rest assured, (13) it's perfectly normal to feel the way you do, (14) and you are certainly not doing any harm in exercising that torrid imagination. (15) For the sake of your husband's ego, however, I would think twice about telling him.

Though not identical, the generic structure is very close to that of 1.1:

Confessional narrative (1–3)
↓
Request for advice (4–5)
↓
Discussion: analysis of the general
problem distilled from the narrative (6–11)
↓
Adhortation: solution of the problem
in the form of advice (12–15)

When a structure of this kind is used in a news article, as in the case of our first example, an additional factor enters the picture. Most of the speech acts have a *double* structure, because they are "projected." If one regards the projecting clauses (clauses like "Mark, aged six," "Valerie says," etc.) as the main clauses, the speech acts are *reports* of what "Mark" and "Valerie" said, and the structure becomes a fairly loose concatenation of reported sayings. As a result, the piece can be read in terms of two discursive practices, as a journalistic report and as a piece of expert guidance.

## 5. Transformations

What happens, what kinds of transformations take place in the process of recontextualization? This is the major concern of this book, and here I can only give a first approximation.

### (1) Substitutions

The most fundamental transformation is the substitution of elements of the actual social practice with semiotic elements. As soon as this happens, new meanings are added, though in some cases more drastically than in others. In example 1.1, for instance, some participants are *particularized* and *nominated* (e.g., "Mark," Valerie"), others *generalized* and *aggregated* ("large numbers of children"), and some actions are *objectivated* through nominalization (e.g., "separation from families"), while others are *spatialized* (e.g., "the classroom situation").

What kinds of substitution occur depends on the context *into* which a practice is recontextualized. Our example text, for instance, *particularizes* what parents do and *generalizes* and *objectivates* what teachers do, perhaps because the text is addressing parents/readers from a position which is ultimately derived from, and aligned with, the practices of the social institution of education (Valerie Martin, the principal source, is a "teacher-turned-author"). As such, the text withholds from parents any detailed knowledge of "what teachers do," of what goes on inside school. It keeps the parents outside of the school gate, so to speak. Again, the article *nominates* when, to draw in the reader, it tells the story of Mark, and also when it fulfills its reporting function (e.g., "when Mum took me to school," "Valerie says") because both narration and reporting are oriented toward concrete, specific events, though in different ways: where reporting presents a world of disconnected, isolated events, morsels of fact, narration presents a world of causally linked events that culminate in a logical outcome, a resolution. On the other hand, the article *generalizes* in Valerie's exposition of "the problems," because the expertise of experts consists in knowing how to recognize similarities and patterns in events, and how to predict events on that basis. In the world of the expert, abstract concepts and issues are the real, "personalizations," "dramatizations," and so on are the transformations, while in the world of the journalist and the storyteller specific people and events and places are the real and generalizations, abstractions, etc., the transformations. It is an opposition with deep religious and philosophical roots in our culture which has, on the one hand, the heritage of the Hebrew God who is known by what he does (lead the Israelites out of

Egypt, send his son, and so on) and, on the other hand, the heritage of Plato, of the timeless, abstract, and universal essence behind the manifold appearances, a heritage which led to a God who *is* rather than a God who *does*.

## (2) Deletions

Recontextualization may also involve the deletion of elements of the social practice.

In 1.1, for instance, the participant "teacher" has been deleted as a result of nominalization ("separation from families"): the parent/reader is not told who does the separating, at least not explicitly, and this stresses the boundary between the domain of the family and the domain of school: the parent is not allowed in, not allowed to know exactly what goes on in school.

Generalized names for whole activity sequences, or large portions thereof (e.g., "getting ready for the first day" or "the first day itself") do not necessarily imply deletion. The detailed activities may be referred to elsewhere in the text. When this is not the case, however, they cause the detail to be deleted. It may be that such detail is readily supplied by the reader (e.g., the deletion of the "resources" involved in "cleaning your teeth") so that its inclusion would seem condescending. It may also be that detail is withheld for other reasons. In our example, the practices of researching and writing a book are not referred to in detail perhaps because they are deemed irrelevant to *Daily Mirror* readers. In other contexts (e.g., research reports), such detail *is* usually supplied. When "experts" address other "experts," for instance, their credibility depends on it. But when they address the "public" (usually mediated by journalists) the mystique of expertise is considered sufficient proof, and the activities of the experts are not disclosed in any detail. The public ends up with a vague and woolly knowledge of these activities, and is therefore likely to reify their results beyond the possibility of critique.

## (3) Rearrangements

Elements of the social practice, insofar as they have a necessary order, may be rearranged, scattered through the text in various ways. In our example text, for instance, the activity of "preparing for the first day" comes after the activity of "taking the child to school," when, in reality, the two would have to occur in reverse order. Again, "separation from families" follows "really love school," when in reality the opposite order would have to apply.

Such rearrangements are motivated by the concerns of the recontextualizing practice: the generic structure of the article, with its stages of "drawing the reader in," "explaining the problem," and "providing the solutions in the form of adhortations to parents" necessitates them. The activities are rearranged to suit the persuasive and hortatory purposes which constitute them as a social practice.

## (4) Additions

Elements can also be added to the recontextualized social practice.

*Repetitions*

The same element may occur a number of times in the text. In example 1.1, we have, for instance:

From the point of view of reference (see Halliday and Hasan, 1976), this is a series of repetitions, a series of synonyms, but when, as in this example, different expressions are used to refer to the same element of a social practice, substitution and the addition of new elements are also involved. New angles, new semantic features are added each time a new expression is used, gradually building up a more multifaceted concept. An ongoing *concept formation* takes place, with the resulting concept fusing the semantic features of all of the expressions used as synonyms. In the above example, this adds, for instance, an element of evaluation ("the big day") to the recontextualization of "starting school."

*Reactions*

Like many other texts, our example text includes (some of) the participants' subjective reactions to the activities that make up the social practice (Mark "starts to cry," children "can become unsettled," and so on). It is not immediately clear whether these should be seen as part of the structure of the social practice itself, or as elements added in the recontextualization. On the one hand, reactions can often be related to the concerns of a recontextualizing social practice. Radical antischooling texts, such as Illich's *Deschooling Society* (1973), a text to which I will return in more detail later, include many negative reactions of both children and parents, while elsewhere, e.g., in 1.1, reactions are positive ("happy," "memorable"). Negative reactions, such as those of Mark when "Mum first takes him to school," are particularized and seen as problematic. "Worry" is discouraged.

On the other hand, reactions may also be behavioralized, and in that case they become actions in their own right. The performance of a social practice may require that participants smile, or look solemn, or even cry, as in the funeral rites of many societies. What matters here is not what the participants really feel—such "real feelings," if they figure in the text, can be considered elements added in the recontextualization—what matters is whether or not the participants act out their feelings in accordance with social expectations or not.

## Purposes

The purposes of the same social practice may be constructed differently in different recontextualizations of the same practice. An "antischooling" text might construct the purpose of texts such as example 1.1 as obtaining parents' complicity with the school system, against their better interests. A "proschooling" text might see them as helping to smooth the inevitable transition between home and school. Our example text itself is silent about its purpose. It is not silent, however, about the purposes of the social practices it recontextualizes. The purpose of "getting ready for the first day," for instance, is explicitly provided: "to take the hassle out of the first day."

Purposes, then, are not intrinsic parts of activities or activity sequences, at least not in ways that can be known explicitly. They are *added* to activities and activity sequences in discourse. And, as such, they are often the stuff of controversy and debate.

## Legitimations

Apart from the "what for," the purpose, recontextualizations may also add the "why" to their representations of social practices, that is, they may add legitimations, reasons that either the whole of a social practice or some part of it must take place, or must take place in the way that it does. Texts not only represent social practices, they also explain and legitimate (or delegitimate, critique) them. The legitimations in 1.1, for instance, are either "psychological," founded on the expert author's special knowledge of the needs and feelings of children (e.g., parents must "get everything ready" because "children become unsettled if they have to rush"), or pieces of stoic, commonsense wisdom such as "it won't last long."

The same social practices, or parts thereof, may be legitimized in different ways, depending on the concerns of the recontextualizing practice. "Getting ready," for instance, might also be legitimized by an appeal to tradition ("that's how my mother did it") rather than to expert psychological knowledge. And the same legitimation discourses may serve to legitimate different social practices. "Child psychology," for instance, can also be used in family counseling education, in the publishing industry (rules for writing and illustrating books aimed at certain age groups), and so on. Domains of knowledge used for legitimizing or delegitimizing social practices have specific distributions across recontextualizing practices, determined by the social relations that obtain in the recontextualizing social practices (e.g., class and gender differences) and the nature of the practices that are being recontextualized (e.g., whether or not they involve children).

The role of legitimation in texts may vary in importance. Some texts are almost entirely about legitimation or delegitimation, and make only rudimentary reference to the social practices they legitimize or delegitimize. In other texts, legitimation plays a minor role, or is absent altogether. The relative paucity of legitimations in example 1.1 perhaps shows that the practice of "getting children ready for the first day" is regarded here as essentially common sense and in little need of legitimation. This of course makes this kind of text all the more important to study. Commonsense practices are the most deeply ideological of all, and it often turns out that they were hotly debated when they first became institutionalized. The "genesis amnesia" (Bourdieu,

1977: 23) which has since taken place is no doubt itself a mechanism of legitimation, enacted in the practices of education and training, and, as Bourdieu notes:

> by the objectivist apprehension which, grasping the product of history as an *opus operatum*, a fait accompli, can only invoke the mysteries of preestablished harmony or the prodigies of conscious orchestration to account for...the coherence of works or institutions such as myths, rites or bodies of law. (1977: 79)

*Evaluation*

Finally, recontextualizations may add evaluations to elements of social practice, or to social practices (or parts of them) as a whole. In themselves, such judgments are not legitimations, and they may appear in texts without being further legitimized. Yet they are ultimately always connected with legitimations. In this there is, however, a difference between "morally good" and "morally bad" and other kinds of "good" and "bad," for instance, functionally good ("useful," "handy," etc.), aesthetically good ("beautiful," "elegant," etc.), emotionally good ("exciting," "satisfying," etc.). "Morally good" necessarily bears a relation to a legitimizing discourse—the laws instituted by God, the laws of nature, the laws of society, or some combination thereof. This applies also to such common evaluations as "innovative," "big," "progressive," and so on, which relate to the normative discourse of continuous progress toward bigger and better things that underpins so many of our institutions. Other kinds of "good" and "bad," on the other hand, refer back to the social practices themselves. A tool is "useful" because it allows a certain activity. An activity is "useful" because it allows the achievement of a certain goal, or "exciting" because it allows a certain reaction. In other words, while a legitimizing discourse is needed to legitimize "moral evaluations," other evaluations are legitimized by the practice itself, or by the purposes or reactions connected to it in a given recontextualizing practice. In the latter case, evaluation circumvents morality and cannot be further legitimized other than in a circular fashion. Which kinds of evaluation will occur in a particular recontextualizing social practice will, again, depend on the concerns and values connected to that practice. In journalistic reporting, evaluations are, in the main, comparatively rare. Example 1.1 has some "emotional" evaluations, realized by lexical items with an evaluative connotation ("hassle," "unsettled"), in a context which suggests ways of avoiding these negative emotions. On the evaluative aspects of the adjective "big," I have already commented when discussing concept formation.

There is, of course, also an evaluative element in reactions, since these can be seen as forming a spectrum that runs from positive to negative. However, reactions are expressed or felt by participants of the recontextualized practice, rather than expressed by the agent of an alternative recontextualization of the practice, which may be quoted or reported within a recontextualization.

## 6. Structure of the Book

The remainder of this book describes how the elements of social practices discussed in this chapter can be, and are, transformed in the process of recontextualization.

It provides "grammars" of recontextualization which show in detail how, for instance, the timing or the legitimation of social practices can be represented in discourse, and it provides critical analyses of the ways in which these grammars are actually used.

For the most part, I focus on the linguistic realizations of the categories I introduce. But it is clear that other semiotic modes can also recontextualize social practices. In the last two chapters, I work out in detail how social actors can be represented visually and in Playmobil, a toy "system" which could be said to provide a systematic description of the social world. Other chapters, too, will occasionally introduce nonlinguistic examples.

Throughout, the critical relevance of the categories I introduce is of crucial importance to me. To take as an example the chapter on recontextualizing the timing of social practices, timing is clearly a key aspect of the organization of social life, and deciding when and for how long things will be done is a particularly powerful role: think, for instance, of the "countdown" to the latest war in Iraq. It is therefore important that the "grammar" of timing presented in chapter 4 will be a useful tool for the critical analysis of the representation of specific instances and practices of timing.

Clearly, the project of this book is not yet complete. There are, for instance, no chapters yet on performance modes, presentation styles, material resources, or eligibility conditions, and a great deal of further work is possible on the nonlinguistic representation of social practices. I hope that the work presented in this book will be a useful tool for critical discourse analysis, but I also, and above all, hope that it will be extended, critiqued, and developed further.

# Representing Social Actors

In this chapter, I investigate how the *participants* of social practices can be represented in English discourse. Since in an earlier version of this chapter, I used the term "social actor" rather than "participant," and since my use of this term has now gained some currency, I will retain the term "social actor" here.

## 1. A Sociosemantic Inventory

My question, "How can social actors be represented in English?" is a grammatical question if, with Halliday, we take a grammar to be a "meaning potential" ("what *can* be said") rather than a set of rules ("what *must* be said"). Yet, unlike many other linguistically oriented forms of critical discourse analysis, I will not start out from linguistic operations, such as nominalization and passive agent deletion, or from linguistic categories, such as the categories of transitivity, but instead will draw up a *sociosemantic* inventory of the ways in which social actors can be represented and establish the sociological and critical relevance of my categories before I turn to the question of how they are realized linguistically.

There are two reasons for doing so. The first stems from the lack of bi-uniqueness of language. Agency, for instance, as a sociological concept, is of major and classic importance in critical discourse analysis: in which contexts are which social actors represented as "agents" and which as "patients"? But sociological agency is not always realized by linguistic agency, by the grammatical role of "agent": it can also be realized in many other ways, for instance, by possessive pronouns (as in "our intake of migrants") or by a prepositional phrase with "from," as in example 2.1, in which the grammatical agent is sociologically "patient":

2.1 People of Asian descent say they received a sudden cold-shoulder from neighbours and co-workers.

There is no neat fit between sociological and linguistic categories, and if critical discourse analysis, e.g., in investigating agency, ties itself too closely to specific linguistic operations or categories, many relevant instances of agency might be overlooked. One cannot, it seems, have it both ways with language. Either theory and method are formally neat but semantically messy (as in the dictionary: one form, many meanings), or they are semantically neat but formally messy (as in the thesaurus: one concept, many possible realizations). Linguists tend toward preserving the unity of formal categories. I will try here for the opposite approach.

Halliday (1985: ch. 10) has approached the problem of the lack of bi-uniqueness in another way, through his theory of grammatical metaphor: certain linguistic realizations are "literal" or "congruent," others "metaphorical" or "incongruent." But in Halliday's account, "congruent" would seem to mean "congruent with the grammatical system," rather than "congruent with reality," the kind of congruence which, ultimately, underlies most definitions of metaphor. For Halliday, a clause like "the report confirms…" would not be a metaphor, because it does not violate the criterion that verbal processes do not require a human "sayer" as their subject (cf. Halliday, 1985: 129). I would prefer to see "the report confirms…" as just one of the ways in which we can refer to social actors in their role as "sayers," as metaphorical or unmetaphorical as any other way, but endowed with its own sociosemantic import and hence social distribution: it is likely to be found in contexts where the authority of utterances is bound up with the official status or role of "sayers" and/or genres. In the context of literature, on the other hand, it would be less likely to occur, because there the authority of utterances is bound up with the charismatic personality of the writer, so that we would expect "T. S. Eliot says…" rather than "the poem says…," for instance. I would therefore prefer to ask: how can the agents of verbal processes be represented—impersonally or personally, individually or collectively, by reference to their person or their utterance, etc.—without privileging any of these choices as more "literal" than others, and without thereby also privileging the context or contexts in which one or the other tends to occur as more normative than others?

The second reason is somewhat different and follows from the assumption that meanings belong to culture rather than to language and cannot be tied to any specific semiotic. Language can represent social actions impersonally, as in this headline:

2.2 Allied air activity over battlefield intensifies.

But so can pictures—think of the difference between, on the one hand, "personalized" pictures of bombardments, say in feature film sequences showing, in close-up, the faces of the crew as they drop the bombs and the faces of the villagers down below as they are about to be bombed, and, on the other hand, diagrams of the same event, for instance, maps with large arrows pointing at the targets and schematic drawings representing the explosions. I will return to this in more detail in chapters 8 and 9. For the moment, it is enough to say that the categories I will propose in this chapter should, in principle, be seen as pan-semiotic: a given culture (or a given context within a culture) has not only its own, specific array of ways of representing the social world, but also its own specific ways of mapping the different semiotic modes onto this array, or prescribing, with greater or lesser strictness, what can be realized verbally and visually, what only verbally, what only visually, and so on. And these arrangements will also be subject to historical change, sometimes even violent change, as in iconoclasms. The point is important for critical discourse analysis for, with the increasing use of visual representation in a wide range of contexts, it becomes more and more pressing to be able to ask the same critical questions with regard to both verbal and visual representations, indeed, with regard to representations in all of the "media" that form parts of contemporary "multimedia" texts.

Despite this, my account of the representation of social actors in this chapter will be grounded in linguistics. Each of the representational choices I propose will be tied to specific linguistic or rhetorical realizations. To return to my earlier examples, in the case of "T. S. Eliot," the representational choice is that of nomination, and the realization the use of a proper name, while in the case of "the report confirms..." the representational choice is that of "utterance autonomization" and the realization the substitution of the utterance for its sayer, hence a form of metonymical reference. The difference is that my primary focus is on sociological categories ("nomination," "agency," etc.) rather than on linguistic categories ("nominalization," "passive agent deletion," etc.) and that the system network I will present below will range over a variety of linguistic and rhetorical phenomena, finding its unity in the concept of "social actor" rather than in a linguistic concept such as, for instance, the "nominal group."

## 2. "Our Race Odyssey"

Below, I reproduce the first three sections of "Our Race Odyssey," the text from which I will draw many of my examples in this and the next chapter, and which I will use to demonstrate how the categories I propose may be used in the critical analysis of racist discourse. The text was published as the leading feature article in "Spectrum," the Saturday supplement of the *Sydney Morning Herald*, a conservative broadsheet newspaper, on 12 May 1990. In addition, I will use examples from my "first day at school" corpus.

1. 2001: Our Race Odyssey.
2. This country will be vastly different next century if Australians feel they cannot voice legitimate fears about immigration, argues David Jenkins.
3. In Florence last month 80 young white thugs, many wearing costume masks and armed with iron bars, roamed the narrow cobbled streets attacking African street vendors.
4. In France, where non-European immigrants make up 6.5 percent of the population, former president Valéry Giscard d'Estaing proposed a total halt to immigration.
5. In Japan, a nation with a strong tradition of keeping foreigners at arm's length, similar concerns are being expressed about a mere trickle of Third World immigrants.

6. Japan's National Police Agency had to apologise recently for circulating an internal memo to police stations claiming that Pakistanis working in Japan "have a unique body odour," carry infectious skin diseases and tell lies "under the name of Allah."

7. The mayor of Kawaguchi has "joked" that with so many dark-skinned foreigners in town, Japanese are having trouble seeing them at night.

8. In Peru, where the son of Japanese immigrants is a presidential front-runner, the situation is reversed.

9. A racist backlash against ethnic Asians has been unleashed by those who resent the prominence of centrist candidate Alberto Fujimoro.

10. People of Asian descent say they have been insulted in the street, denied entry to elegant restaurants, and received a sudden cold-shoulder from neighbours and co-workers.

11. In Canada, where the 250,000-strong Sikh community has pressed for the right to have Mounties in turbans and where 22,000 Hong Kong Chinese arrived last year, bringing bulging wallets to cities like Vancouver, racial tolerance is wearing thin.

12. "Native Vancouverites will be made to feel like strangers in their own city as the influx of Asians and their capital freezes them out," wrote one reader of the *Province* newspaper in Vancouver.

13. If you were sitting in Canberra and doing no more than reading the daily newspapers you would be entitled to be a bit concerned by these developments.

14. They italicise the lesson that people, whatever their race, display their less attractive characteristics when they feel threatened and unable to cope with rapid change in the society around them.

15. They highlight the fact that racism is seldom far below the surface—whether it is in Western Europe, in Asia, in North or South America.

16. They may even call into question some aspects of Australia's immigration programme, which is now running at close to record levels, with annual net migration of about 150,000, including 60,000 migrants from Asia.

17. Is the Australian government concerned?

18. Not a bit.

19. Prime Minister Bob Hawke says he is "philosophically" a high-migration man.

20. He thinks our current intake is about right.

21. "I hope that as we go on," he said recently, "that we may be able to look at higher levels of immigration."

22. Is the Prime Minister entitled to be quite so confident that we have got our immigration policy settings right?

23. Is he entitled to believe that this nation, which only recently shed the White Australia Policy, is somehow impervious to racist sentiment?

24. On the evidence to date there is some reason to suppose that he is.
25. We have had one of the most successful immigration programmes in the world.
26. Forty percent of Australians were born overseas or have at least one parent who was born overseas; in Sydney, the figure is 49 percent.
27. We have become one of the most diverse groups of people in the world.
28. We have achieved all this with remarkably little disharmony or dislocation.
29. We are entitled to be proud—not apologetic—about our immigration programme.
30. We are entitled to be resentful about the damaging distortions that are presented as fact by Bruce Roxton, who spent the major part of his three-year military career as an army cook, when he marches into TV studios in Singapore and Hong Kong.
31. We have avoided most of the problems that bedevil Western Europe because few of our non-European migrants have been poor, black, unskilled, Muslim, or illegal.
32. They have tended to be Asian and they tended to come, at least until recently, from an educated elite that was English-speaking and middle-class.
33. However, all that is changing.
34. Migration from traditional source countries like Italy and Greece has dried up.
35. Migration from the Third World, especially Asia and the Middle East, is becoming increasingly important.
36. And though many of the new migrants are educated high-achievers from places like Singapore and Hong Kong—"uptown" people in American terminology—others are "downtown" people from places like Vietnam, the Philippines and Lebanon.
37. The "downtown" migrants tend to be unskilled or low-skilled, tend to have high unemployment rates—Lebanese, Turks and Vietnamese have unemployment rates three to four times the national average—and tend to be significant users of social welfare.
38. With these changes is coming a change in community attitudes.
39. Many Australians, the 1988 Fitzgerald Committee reported, were "bewildered" by the changing face of Australia.
40. They did not feel they understood or could influence this change.
41. They felt "besieged" by immigration.
42. They believed that the immigration programme existed for the benefit of politicians, bureaucrats, and the ethnic minorities, not for Australians as a whole.
43. This concern, the report noted, was reflected in surveys which showed that the level of support for stopping immigration altogether was at a post-war high.

44. If you stop for a moment and consider all this you will see that there is something very odd going on.
45. On the one hand we have a Prime Minister who says he is philosophically disposed to high migration, a Prime Minister who has been presiding over a near record intake of migrants.
46. On the other we have public support for immigration at an all-time low.
47. This suggests a yawning gap between what people think about immigration and what politicians and other community leaders feel they can or should say about immigration.
48. It is hardly surprising therefore that the immigration debate is building again.
49. Hardly surprising that there are calls for major cuts in the programme.
50. Hardly surprising that a number of critics wants to see our intake halved to 70,000 to 80,000, which would bring it into line with our post-war average.
51. Australia, these critics suggest, is being generous to a fault—and in danger of saddling itself with a lot of unwanted problems as a result.

## 3. Exclusion

The "Race Odyssey" text draws on a representation of the social practice of immigration itself, as institutionalized in Australia, as well as on the representation of other social practices which serve to legitimize (or delegitimize) it: the practices of writing government-commissioned reports on immigration, or of conducting public opinion surveys about it, for instance. All of these practices involve specific sets of social actors, but a given representation such as the "Race Odyssey" text will include some of these actors, for instance Prime Minister Bob Hawke, who "presides over a near record intake of migrants," and will exclude others, for instance, the people who "brand as racist" those who "voice legitimate fears about immigration." Representations include or exclude social actors to suit their interests and purposes in relation to the readers for whom they are intended. Some of the exclusions may be "innocent," details which readers are assumed to know already, or which are deemed irrelevant to them; others tie in closely to the propaganda strategies of creating fear and of setting up immigrants as enemies of "our" interests.

Exclusion has rightly been an important aspect of critical discourse analysis. To mention just one classic example, Tony Trew (1979: 97ff.) showed how, in the *Times* and the *Rhodesian Herald* (during the year 1975), the police were excluded in accounts of the "riots" during which they had opened fire and killed demonstrators, because it was in the interest of these papers and their readers to attempt to "justify white rule in Africa" and this required

a suppression of the fact that the white regimes apply violence and intimidation, and suppression of the nature of the exploitation this makes possible. It requires that the regimes and their agents be put constantly in the role of promoters of progress, law and order, concerned to eliminate social evil and conflict, but never responsible for it. (Trew, 1979: 106)

Some exclusions leave no traces in the representation, excluding both the social actors and their activities. Such radical exclusion can play a role in a critical comparison of different representations of the same social practice, but not in an analysis of a single text, for the simple reason that it leaves no traces behind. In my "first day at school" texts, for instance, fathers are radically excluded in texts addressing teachers, but are included in many children's stories, even if often only briefly, during the breakfast preceding the first school day, or as givers of satchels, pencil cases, and other school necessities. Children's stories aimed at a mass market sometimes include school support staff, but exclude the principal, while more "upmarket" children's stories include the principal but exclude people lower than teachers in the school hierarchy, in what is clearly a class-related pattern of inclusion and exclusion (Van Leeuwen, 1993b).

When the relevant actions (e.g., the killing of demonstrators) are included, but some or all of the actors involved in them (e.g., the police) are excluded, the exclusion *does* leave a trace. We can ask "But who did the killing?" or "But who was killed?" even though the text does not provide the answers. In this case, a further distinction should perhaps be made, the distinction between *suppression* and *backgrounding*. In the case of suppression, there is no reference to the social actor(s) in question anywhere in the text. Thus we learn, in the "Race Odyssey" text, that someone or some institution surveyed the opinions of the public, but we do not find out which individual or company or other institution did this, which takes away one possible avenue of contesting the result of these "surveys." In the case of backgrounding, the exclusion is less radical: the excluded social actors may not be mentioned in relation to a given action, but they are mentioned elsewhere in the text, and we can infer with reasonable (though never total) certainty who they are. They are not so much excluded as deemphasized, pushed into the background.

How is suppression realized? First there is, of course, the classic realization through passive agent deletion. Example 2.3 tells us that "concerns are being expressed," but not who expresses them:

2.3  In Japan similar concerns are being expressed about a mere trickle of Third World immigrants.

Suppression can also be realized through nonfinite clauses which function as a grammatical participant. In example 2.4, the infinitival clause "to maintain this policy" is embedded to function as the carrier of an attributive clause, and this allows the social actor(s) responsible for the "maintenance" of the policy to be excluded—and they *could* have been included by adding, for instance, "for local education authorities." The downgrading of the process ("maintain") makes the fact that exclusion has taken place a little less accessible; the trace is a little less clear:

2.4  To maintain this policy is hard.

It is almost always possible to delete "beneficiaries," social actors who benefit from an action. Example 2.5, for instance, does not include those to whom the "National Police Agency" apologized (the Pakistanis who had been offended?):

> 2.5 Japan's National Police Agency had to apologise recently for circulating an internal memo to police stations claiming that Pakistanis working in Japan "have a unique body odour," carry infectious skin diseases and tell lies "under the name of Allah."

Nominalizations and process nouns similarly allow the exclusion of social actors. "Support" and "stopping," in example 2.6, function as nominals, although they refer to actions. The same applies to "immigration." Again, the excluded social actors could have been included, for instance, through postmodifying phrases with *by*, *of*, *from*, etc., but they haven't been:

> 2.6 The level of support for stopping immigration altogether was at a post-war high.

Processes may also be realized as adjectives, as is the case with "legitimate" in example 2.7. Who "legitimizes" the "fear"? The writer? We cannot be sure. The fears simply *are* legitimate, according to this representation:

> 2.7 Australians feel they cannot voice legitimate fears about immigration.

The action in example 2.8 involves a human actor, the teacher who opens the door. But coding the action in the middle voice (Halliday, 1985: 150–51) necessitates the exclusion of the agentive participant. The context may lead us to infer that the teacher was involved, but there can be no certainty—it might, for instance, have been the wind. The clause invites a reading in which the opening of the door and the intrusion of the teacher in the child's world of play are given the force of an unavoidable natural event:

> 2.8 The door of the playhouse opened, and the teacher looked in.

It is often difficult to know whether suppressed social actors are or are not supposed to be retrievable by the reader or, indeed, the writer. Example 2.6, for instance, does not tell us who is involved in the act of "stopping immigration." Is this because readers are assumed to know already, so that more detailed reference would be over-communicative, or is it to block access to knowledge of a practice which, if represented in detail, might arouse compassion for those who are "stopped"? The point is that the practice is here represented as something not to be further examined or contested.

Backgrounding can result from simple ellipses in nonfinite clauses with *-ing* and *-ed* participles, in infinitival clauses with *to*, and in paratactic clauses. In all of these cases, the excluded social actor is *in*cluded elsewhere in the same clause or clause complex. It can also be realized in the same way as suppression, but with respect to social actors who *are* included elsewhere in the text. The two realizations background social actors to different degrees, but both play a part in reducing the number of times specific social actors are explicitly referred to.

To discuss the pattern of inclusion and exclusion in the "Race Odyssey" text, it is necessary to bring the various ways in which each category of social actor is represented under a common denominator. These common denominators do not, of course, form a more transparent or congruent way of referring to them. They merely serve as an anchor for the analysis, a kind of calibration. For the purposes of analysis, then, I shall call "racists" those social actors who, actively or otherwise, oppose immigration and immigrants in countries other than Australia, and I shall refer to those who do the same in Australia as "us." Again, this is not to say that the latter are not racist, but merely to follow the distinction that underlies the way the author argues his case. I shall refer to the immigrants themselves as "them," to the (Australian) government as "government," to the various experts invoked by the writer as "experts," to the writer himself as "writer," and to his readers, who are sometimes addressed directly, as "addressees." Bruce Roxton, the "racist" Australians love to hate, is a category of his own ("our racist"), and finally there are a few minor characters who appear only once, the "antiracists" who "brand as racist" the "legitimate fears of Australians," "Allah," "European governments," and (Japanese) "police stations." Table 2.1 displays some of the patterns of inclusion and exclusion.

Although the differences are not dramatic, it is clear that the most frequently included social actors are the Australian government and "us" Australians, who voice "legitimate fears," while the most frequently backgrounded or suppressed social actors are, on the one hand, the immigrants and, on the other hand, those in other countries who commit such racist acts as "insulting" and "denying entry to elegant restaurants," and, indeed, people in general, as they are "naturally inclined to racism" and will "display unpleasant characteristics when they feel threatened." In short, those who do not take part in the "debate" between the Australian people and its government, which the writer stages for us in his arguments, form to some extent a backdrop to this debate.

Although counting frequencies can reveal significant patterns, I do not want to make great claims for numbers. On the contrary, it is important to realize that frequencies often shift with the stages in the writer's argument and may not be an overall characteristic of the text. In the first section of the text, where the writer discusses racism

TABLE 2.1. Inclusion and Exclusion in the "Race Odyssey" Text

|  | Included % | Backgrounded % | Suppressed % |
|---|---|---|---|
| "racists" (N = 24) | 67.25 | 20.25 | 12.5 |
| "us" (N = 46) | 72 | 24 | 4 |
| "them" (N = 98) | 61 | 38 | 1 |
| "government" (N = 32) | 73 | 18 | 9 |

in other countries, migrants are backgrounded in 17 percent of the cases. As soon as the writer moves to his discussion of Australian immigration policy, this increases to 36 percent. In other words, the migrants close to home are backgrounded more often. In any case, the patterns of inclusion and exclusion must be integrated with the way in which they are represented, which I shall discuss in the remainder of this chapter.

What, finally, remains most opaque in this text? First, the voice of the opposition: those who "brand as racist" Australians who "voice legitimate fears" are fully suppressed. Second, many of the "racists" in other countries: we are not told who exactly is responsible for "insulting people of Asian descent" or "denying them entry to elegant restaurants," for example. Third, the voice of legitimation, which "legitimizes fears" and "entitles" Hawke and "us" to the views which, by virtue of their sheer prominence in the text, the writer obliquely favors. And finally, those who have to do the dirty work of actually "stopping" ("halting," "cutting," etc.) the immigrants.

## 4. Role Allocation

I shall now consider the roles that social actors are given to play in representations, an aspect of representation which also plays a significant part in the work of many critical linguists (e.g., Fairclough, 1989a; Fowler, 1991; Fowler et al., 1979; Kress and Hodge, 1979; Van Dijk, 1991): who is represented as "agent" ("actor"), who as "patient" ("goal") with respect to a given action? This question remains important, for there need not be congruence between the roles that social actors actually play in social practices and the grammatical roles they are given in texts. Representations can reallocate roles or rearrange the social relations between the participants. Here are two examples from the field of television studies:

2.9   Children seek out aspects of commercial television as a consolidation and confirmation of their everyday lives.... The kids use it [television] subversively against the rule-bound culture and institution of the school. (Curthoys and Docker, 1989: 68)

2.10  Television affects children's sex-role attitudes.... Furthermore, television has been shown to influence more subtle areas such as racial attitudes and cultural views. (Tuchman et al., 1978: 232)

Leaving aside aspects of the representation of social actors we have not yet discussed (objectivations such as "television" and "subtle areas"; abstractions such as "aspects of commercial television") and the exclusions (e.g., in "racial attitudes and cultural views"), the two major categories of social actor represented are "children" and "television." In example 2.9, "children" and "the kids" are, grammatically, the actor in relation to actions such as "seeking out" and "using" (and also, if one ignores the backgrounding, of "consolidating" and "confirming"), while "television" ("aspects of commercial television" and "it") is the goal of both of these processes. In 2.10, "television" is actor of "affect" and "influence," while "children" ("children's sex-role attitudes," "subtle areas such as racial attitudes and cultural views") are goal. In other words, in one of the representations (that of a populist, "active audience" theory), the active role is given to children, the passive role to television, while in the other (that of the "effects," or "hypodermic needle" theory of mass communication), the active role is given to television and the passive role to children. The two examples deal, in the end, with the same reality, but which of them corresponds best to that reality is of course a problem that text analysis cannot solve. What we can do, however, is investigate which options are chosen in which institutional and social contexts, and why these choices should have been made, what interests are served by them, and what purposes achieved.

I shall say, then, that representations can endow social actors with either active or passive roles. *Activation* occurs when social actors are represented as the active, dynamic forces in an activity, *passivation* when they are represented as "undergoing" the activity, or as being "at the receiving end of it." This may be realized by grammatical participant roles, by transitivity structures in which activated social actors are coded as actor in material processes, behaver in behavioral processes, senser in mental processes, sayer in verbal processes, or assigner in relational processes (Halliday, 1985: ch. 5). In 2.11, for example, "they" (i.e., "us," Australians) are actor in relation to the process of "feeling," but "immigration" (i.e., "immigrants," "them") is activated in relation to "besieging." In 2.12, on the other hand, "young white thugs" are activated and "African street vendors" passivated. In other words, while in other countries there may be active racists, in Australia the migrants play the active (and "threatening") role, and "we" are at best activated as "sensers" in mental processes such as "feeling."

2.11 They felt "besieged" by immigration.
2.12 [Eighty] young white thugs attacked African street vendors.

When, as in these cases, activation is realized by "participation" (grammatical participant roles), the active role of the social actor in question is most clearly foregrounded; note how, in examples 2.9 and 2.10, active roles are realized by participation, passive roles in other, more highly transformed ways. But activation can also be realized in other ways, for example, through "circumstantialization," that is, by prepositional circumstantials with *by* or *from*, as with "from neighbours and co-workers" in

2.13 People of Asian descent suddenly received a cold-shoulder from neighbours and co-workers.

Premodification (e.g., "public" in "public support") or postmodification (e.g., "of Asians" in "the influx of Asians") of nominalizations or process nouns can also realize activation. A frequent form of this is "possessivation," the use of a possessive pronoun to activate (e.g., "our intake") or passivate (e.g., "my teacher") a social actor. By comparison to participation, this backgrounds agency, changing it into the "possession" of a process which has itself been transformed into a "thing."

Passivation necessitates a further distinction: the passivated social actor can be *subjected* or *beneficialized*. Subjected social actors are treated as objects in the representation, for instance, as objects of exchange (immigrants "taken in" in return for the skill or money they bring). Beneficialized social actors form a third party which, positively or negatively, benefits from the action. In 2.14, for instance, "about 70,000 migrants" are subjected to the action of "bringing in." In 2.15, "cities like Vancouver" are beneficialized in relation to "bringing":

> 2.14  Australia was bringing in about 70,000 migrants a year.
> 2.15  [Twenty-two thousand] Hong Kong Chinese arrived last year, bringing bulging wallets to cities like Vancouver.

There is a cryptogrammatical criterion for considering both of these roles passivations: goals as well as beneficiaries can become subject in passive clauses. But there is of course also a grammatical criterion for distinguishing them: beneficiaries can take a preposition (although they do not have to; see Halliday, 1985: 132ff.), goals generally cannot.

Like activation, subjection can be realized in various ways. It is realized by "participation" when the passivated social actor is goal in a material process, phenomenon in a mental process, or carrier in an effective attributive process (Halliday, 1985: 43): "African street vendors" in 2.12 is an example. It can also be realized by "circumstantialization" through a prepositional phrase with, for instance, *against*, as in 2.16, where "ethnic Asians" are passivated:

> 2.16  A racist backlash against ethnic Asians has been unleashed by those who resent the prominence of centrist candidate Alberto Fujimoro.

And it can also be realized by "possessivation," usually in the form of a prepositional phrase with *of* postmodifying a nominalization or process noun, as with "of some 54,000 skilled immigrants" in 2.17:

> 2.17  An intake of some 54,000 skilled immigrants is expected this year.

Finally, adjectival premodification can also passivate as, for example, with "racial" in "racial tolerance," where (people of different) races are passivated; the example also *abstracts* the social actors represented.

Beneficialization may be realized by participation, in which case the beneficialized participant is recipient or client in relation to a material process, or receiver in relation to a verbal process (Halliday, 1985: 132–33). Table 2.2 shows how the "Race Odyssey" text allocates roles to the most frequently represented social actors.

TABLE 2.2.  Role Allocation in the "Race Odyssey" Text

|  | Activated % | Subjected % | Beneficialized % |
|---|---|---|---|
| "racists" (N = 21) | 81 | 14 | 5 |
| "us" (N = 40) | 85 | 12.5 | 2.5 |
| "them" (N = 66) | 53 | 45 | 2 |
| "government" (N = 29) | 86 | 7 | 7 |

It is clear that "racists," "government," and "us" most often act upon the immi-grants, be it materially or symbolically, and that the immigrants themselves are acti-vated only, or almost only, in relation to one action, the act of immigrating ("influx," "arriving," etc.), and this mostly in nominalized and deeply embedded form.

## 5. Genericization and Specification

The choice between generic and specific reference is another important factor in the representation of social actors; they can be represented as classes, or as specific, identifiable individuals. Compare, for instance, the following two texts:

> 2.18 The reference is specific since we have in mind specific specimens of the class tiger.
> (Quirk et al., 1972: 147)
> 2.19 Classification is an instrument of control in two directions: control over the flux of experience of physical and social reality...and society's control over conceptions of that reality. (Kress and Hodge, 1979: 63)

The first example betrays a view of reality in which generalized essences, classes, constitute the real and in which specific participants are "specimens" of those classes. In the second example, the real is constituted by the "flux of experience," by a spe-cific, concrete world, populated with specific, concrete people, places, things, and actions, and "classification" is seen as an operation upon this reality, which creates a kind of second-order reality, a "conception of reality."

Sociologists have linked such concepts of reality to social class. For Bourdieu (1986), concrete reference to immediate experience is linked to the habitus of the working class, that is, to the principles and values that lie behind their appreciation of art, music, and literature; their moral and political judgments; and so on. "Distance, height, the overview of the observer who places himself above the hurly-burly" (Bourdieu, 1986: 444), on the other hand, are linked to the habitus of the dominant class, the bourgeoisie, and Bourdieu approvingly quotes Virginia Woolf's dictum that "general ideas are always Generals' ideas." From this perspective, he says, spe-cific reference is a "blind, narrow, partial vision" (ibid.). In a similar vein, Bernstein (e.g., 1971: 197) has argued that "elaborated codes" give access to "universalistic orders of meaning," while restricted codes give access to "particularistic orders of meaning," and access to these codes is class determined.

The difference can be observed, for instance, in the way that social actors are represented by different sectors of the press. In middle-class-oriented newspapers, government agents and experts tend to be referred to specifically, and "ordinary peo-ple" generically: the point of identification, the world in which one's specifics exist, is here not the world of the governed, but the world of the governors, the "gener-als." In working-class-oriented newspapers, on the other hand, "ordinary people" are frequently referred to specifically. The following two examples illustrate the dif-ference. They deal with the same topic and the articles from which they were taken appeared on the same day, their news value deriving from the same statement by Australia's minister for sport and recreation. The first comes from the *Sydney Morning*

*Herald*, a middle-class-oriented newspaper, the second from the *Daily Telegraph*, a working-class-oriented newspaper:

> 2.20  Australia has one of the highest childhood drowning rates in the world, with chil-
> dren under 5 making up a quarter of the toll, this is the grim news from government
> studies of Australia's high incidence of drowning. The studies show over 500 people
> drown in Australia every year, with backyard swimming pools the biggest killers for
> children under 15. The Minister for Sport and Recreation, Mr. Brown, said the child-
> hood drowning rate was higher than developed countries such as Britain and the US
> and comparable with many Asian countries. He said children should be encouraged
> to swim and parents should learn resuscitation techniques.
>
> 2.21  The tragic drowning of a toddler in a backyard swimming pool has mystified his
> family. Matthew Harding, two, one of twin boys, had to climb over a one-metre
> "child-proof" fence before he fell into the pool. Mrs. Desley Harding found Matthew
> floating in the pool when she went to call the twins in for tea yesterday. "I have no
> idea how he got in the pool," said Mrs. Harding at her home in Wentworthville South
> today.

Genericization may be realized by the plural without article, as in 2.22:

> 2.22  Non-European immigrants make up 6.5 percent of the population.

And it may also be realized by the singular with the definite article (2.23) or indefinite article (2.24):

> 2.23  Allow the child to cling to something familiar during times of distress.
> 2.24  Maybe a child senses that from her mother.

If mass nouns are used for generic reference to a group of participants, the article will
be absent, but this form can also be used for specific reference: generic reference is
clearly dependent on a complex of factors, including tense. Example 2.25 has been
interpreted as specific mainly because of the absence of habitual or present tense:

> 2.25  Staff in both playgroups and nurseries expressed willingness to supply information
> if asked and regretted that their opinions were not valued more.

The presence of a numerative, finally, has been interpreted as realizing specific
reference.

Even though one expects a certain amount of generic reference in a general
argument, which is what the "Race Odyssey" text purports to be, this does not mean
that all categories of social actor are equally often genericized. "Racists" in other
countries and "them," the immigrants, are genericized most often (32 and 48 percent,
respectively) and so symbolically removed from the readers' world of immediate
experience, treated as distant "others" rather than as people with whom "we" have
to deal in our everyday lives. The "government" and "us," on the other hand, are less
often genericized (17 and 15 percent, respectively).

## 6. Assimilation

Social actors can be referred to as individuals, in which case I shall speak of *individualization*, or as groups, in which case I shall speak of *assimilation*. Given the great value which is placed on individuality in many spheres of our society (and the value placed on conformity in others), these categories are of primary significance in critical discourse analysis. Examples 2.20 and 2.21 already showed that middle-class-oriented newspapers tend to individualize elite persons and assimilate "ordinary people," while working-class-oriented newspapers quite often individualize "ordinary people." My corpus of "first day at school" texts included an item from the ABC (Australian Broadcasting Commission) radio program *Offspring*, which deals with issues of interest to parents. One of the expert panelists in the program made an explicit plea for individualization, but—experts will be experts, and schools schools—individualization was, itself, assimilated. The children, despite the emphasis on difference, were represented as groups:

> 2.26 However you manipulate the age of entry into school, you are always going to
> have the situation where you have children of different kinds of development and
> with different skills coming into a school programme. And the important thing is
> to make sure that the programme is adapted to meet the needs of all these children
> coming in.

I will distinguish two major kinds of assimilation: aggregation and collectivization. The former quantifies groups of participants, treating them as statistics, the latter does not. Aggregation plays a crucial role in many contexts. In our society, the majority rules, not just in contexts in which formal democratic procedures are used to arrive at decisions, but also and especially in others, through mechanisms such as opinion polls, surveys, marketing research, etc. Even legislative reform is increasingly based on "what most people consider legitimate." For this reason, aggregation is often used to regulate practice and to manufacture consensus opinion, even though it presents itself as merely recording facts. Example 2.27 can be seen as an instance of this use of aggregation:

> 2.27 This concern, the report noted, was reflected in surveys which showed that the level
> of support for stopping migration altogether was at a post-war high.

Individualization is realized by singularity and assimilation by plurality, as with "Australians" and "Muslims" in 2.28:

> 2.28 Australians tend to be sceptical about admitting "Muslims."

Alternatively, assimilation may be realized by a mass noun or a noun denoting a group of people as, for instance, with "this nation" in 2.29 and "the community" in 2.30:

> 2.29 Is he [Prime Minister Hawke] entitled to believe that this nation, which only recently
> shed the White Australia Policy, is somehow impervious to racist sentiment?

2.30 The 250,000-strong Sikh community has pressed for the right to have Mounties in turbans.

Aggregation is realized by the presence of definite or indefinite quantifiers which either function as the numerative or as the head of the nominal group, as with "a number of critics" in 2.31 and "forty percent of Australians" in 2.32:

2.31 A number of critics want to see our intake halved to 70,000.

2.32 Forty percent of Australians were born overseas.

The "Race Odyssey" text individualizes "racists" and "immigrants" only when they are also elite persons (Valéry Giscard d'Estaing; the mayor of Kawaguchi; and the presidential candidate, who is the son of immigrants, from Peru, the only "immigrant" in this category). The individualization of racism within Australia, in the person of Bruce Roxton, "our racist," shows that, in the press, notoriety confers as much elite status as does high office.

"We," the people of Australia, are of course mostly collectivized, not only through the first-person plural, but also through terms like "Australia," "this nation," "the community," etc. The government, on the other hand, is mostly individualized—the leader as a strong individual, the people as a homogeneous, consensual group.

"Experts" are collectivized ("the committee," "the surveys"), which helps to signal their agreement. In the remainder of the article, however, they are often individualized, which allows their titles, credentials, and institutional affiliations to be showcased.

As indicated already, immigrants are most frequently aggregated, treated as "statistics," and rather than this being used to realize frequency modality (as in "many Australians"), it makes them not only the subject of "rational" economic calculation, but also makes them that large horde which is so "legitimately feared" by Australians.

## 7. Association and Dissociation

There is another way in which social actors can be represented as groups: *association*. Association, in the sense in which I shall use the term here, refers to groups formed by social actors and/or groups of social actors (either generically or specifically referred to) which are never labeled in the text (although the actors or groups who make up the association may of course themselves be named and/or categorized). The most common realization of association is parataxis, as in this example:

2.33 They believed that the immigration program existed for the benefit of politicians, bureaucrats, and the ethnic minorities, not for Australians as a whole.

Here, "politicians, bureaucrats, and ethnic minorities" are associated to form a group opposed to the interests of "Australians as a whole." But, rather than being represented as stable and institutionalized, the group is represented as an alliance which exists only in relation to a specific activity or set of activities, in this case, their beneficiary role in relation to immigration.

Association may also be realized by "circumstances of accompaniment" (Halliday, 1985: 141), as in

2.34 They played "higher and higher" with the other children.

In this case, the association is, perhaps, even more fleeting and unstable.

Possessive pronouns and possessive attributive clauses with verbs like "have" and "belong" can make an association explicit without naming the resulting social grouping. In this case, however, the association is represented as more stable, enduring, and, indeed, "possessive," as in this example, where "problems" is clearly an abstract reference to a specific kind of immigrant. With other kinds of immigrants, an association may be formed; with this kind of immigrant, it must be "avoided":

2.35 We have avoided most of the problems that bedevil Western Europe because few of our non-European migrants have been poor, black, unskilled, Muslim, or illegal.

In many texts, associations are formed and unformed ("dissociation") as the text proceeds. In one children's story I studied, for instance, there existed, prior to entering school for the first time, an association between two children from the same neighborhood. As they walked to school and shared their worries, they were always referred to as "Mark and Mandy." But the association was disbanded as soon as they entered the classroom. From that moment on, they were referred to either separately or as part of the collective of the "class."

There are only a few associations in the "Race Odyssey" text: the lines between the parties are sharply drawn. Two of the associations lump different ethnic origins together ("Asia and the Middle East," "Lebanese, Turks, and Vietnamese"); another associates the "neighbours and co-workers" who give "ethnic Asians" the cold-shoulder. The cases of "our non-European migrants" and "politicians, bureaucrats, and ethnic minorities" I have already mentioned.

## 8. Indetermination and Differentiation

*Indetermination* occurs when social actors are represented as unspecified, "anonymous" individuals or groups, *determination* when their identity is, one way or another, specified. Indetermination is typically realized by indefinite pronouns ("somebody," "someone," "some," "some people") used in nominal function, as in this example from a children's book, where a member of the school support staff is indeterminated:

2.36 Someone had put flowers on the teacher's desk.

Here, indetermination *anonymizes* a social actor. The writer treats his or her identity as irrelevant to the reader. Indetermination can also be realized by generalized exophoric reference, and in this case it endows social actors with a kind of impersonal authority, a sense of unseen, yet powerfully felt coercive force:

> 2.37  They won't let you go to school until you're five years old.

Indetermination can also be aggregated, as, for example, in "many believe...," "some say...," etc.

Differentiation explicitly differentiates an individual social actor or group of social actors from a similar actor or group, creating the difference between the "self" and the "other," or between "us" and "them," as with "others" in

> 2.38  And though many of the new migrants are educated high-achievers from places like Singapore and Hong Kong—"uptown" people in American terminology, others are "downtown" people from places like Vietnam, the Philippines, and Lebanon.

There are only two cases of this in the "Race Odyssey" text, the one just quoted and the "other community leaders" (i.e., other than "politicians and bureaucrats").

Comparing middle-class-oriented and mass-market-oriented children's stories about the "first day at school" (Van Leeuwen, 1993b), I found that differentiation plays an important role in the former, but does not occur much in the latter. Middle-class children are apparently encouraged to see themselves as individuals, different from "the other children," and much of the trauma of "the first day," as represented in these stories, consists in a kind of identity crisis, the child's discovery that she is not unique:

> 2.39  Mummy, did you know there is another Mary in my class?

The readers of the mass-market-oriented stories, on the other hand, are encouraged to take pleasure in their ability to conform successfully.

## 9. Nomination and Categorization

Social actors can be represented either in terms of their unique identity, by being *nominated*, or in terms of identities and functions they share with others (*categorization*), and it is, again, always of interest to investigate which social actors are, in a given discourse, categorized and which nominated. In stories, for instance, nameless characters fulfill only passing, functional roles and do not become points of identification for the reader or listener. In press "stories," something similar occurs. We saw, for instance, how a middle-class newspaper nominated only a high-status person, a government minister, while a working-class-oriented newspaper, in an article on the same topic, nominated "ordinary people" (examples 2.20 and 2.21). The press (and not only the press) also tends to nominate men and women in different ways, for instance by referring to marital status only in the case of women (example 2.40) or by referring to a female officer as "a captain," rather than as "Captain Carole Maychill" (example 2.42). Both these examples are from the *Guardian*:

2.40  Dwight Harris aged 32...his wife, Beverley, aged 33.
2.41  Carole Maychill, a 32-year-old captain...Colonel Robert Pepper.

Nomination is typically realized by proper nouns, which can be *formal* (surname only, with or without honorifics), *semiformal* (given name and surname, as with "Dwight Harris" in 2.40), or *informal* (given name only, as with Beverley, in 2.40). Occasionally what we might call "name obscuration" occurs: letters or numbers replace names (e.g., "Mr. X") so that nomination can be signified while the name is, at the same time, withheld. All nominations can be used as vocatives and do not occur with a possessive pronoun, except in contexts of special endearment (e.g., "my Cathy")—at least in English, because in other languages the possessive pronoun does not necessarily suggest special endearment (cf. the French "mon Capitaine," "mon Général").

Items other than proper names may be used for nomination, especially when, in a given context, only one social actor occupies a certain rank or fulfills a certain function. Nominations of this kind in fact blur the dividing line between nomination and categorization. They are common in stories for young children, with characters referred to as "the Little Boy," "the Giant," "the Rabbit," etc., even in vocatives:

2.42  Turkish Sultan, give me back my diamond button.

Nominations may be titulated, either in the form of honorification, the addition of standard titles, ranks, etc., as with "Dr." in 2.43, or in the form of affiliations, the addition of personal or kinship relation terms, as with "Auntie Barbara" in 2.44:

2.43  In 50 years, Dr. Price says, 26 percent of the Australian population will be Asian.
2.44  They started out, Auntie Barbara pushing Debbie in her pram.

Press journalists often use what Bell (1985: 98) has called "pseudo titles," such as "controversial cancer therapist Milan Brych." As in standard titles, the definite article is absent in such pseudo titles, but otherwise categorization and nomination are mixed here or, rather, categorizations are used as unique identities, much as in the children's stories quoted above.

The "Race Odyssey" text nominates heads of government (Valéry Giscard d'Estaing, Prime Minister Bob Hawke), "our racist" Bruce Roxton, "experts" (especially in the section that follows the excerpt in section 2 above, where four different experts, all in favor of cutting back immigration, are quoted extensively, nominated, and titulated), and the writer who thereby places himself in high company. Not nominated (absences are as significant in critical discourse analysis as are presences) are "racists" from other countries, "us" Australians, and, of course, the immigrants, with the exception of that high-status immigrants' son, Alberto Fujimoro, the Peruvian presidential candidate.

## 10. Functionalization and Identification

I will distinguish two key types of categorization: *functionalization* and *identification*. Functionalization occurs when social actors are referred to in terms of an activity, in terms of something they do, for instance, an occupation or role. It is typically realized in one of the following ways: first, by a noun, formed from a verb, through suffixes such as *-er, -ant, -ent, -ian, -ee*, e.g., "interviewer," "celebrant," "correspondent," "guardian," "payee"; second, by a noun which denotes a place or tool closely associated with an activity (a noun which, in Halliday's terms [1985: 134ff.] forms the "range of that activity") through suffixes such as *-ist, -eer*, e.g., "pianist," "mountaineer"; third, by the compounding of nouns denoting places or tools closely associated with an activity and highly generalized categorizations, such as "man," "woman," "person," "people" (and, occasionally, functionalizations, such as "assistant"), as in "cameraman," "chairperson."

Identification occurs when social actors are defined, not in terms of what they do, but in terms of what they, more or less permanently, or unavoidably, are. I have distinguished three types: *classification*, *relational identification*, and *physical identification*.

In the case of classification, social actors are referred to in terms of the major categories by means of which a given society or institution differentiates between classes of people. In the West, these now include age, gender, provenance, class, wealth, race, ethnicity, religion, sexual orientation, and so on. But classification categories are historically and culturally variable. What in one period or culture is represented as "doing," as a more or less impermanent role, may in another be represented as "being," as a more or less fixed identity. Foucault (1978) has described how, in the late nineteenth century, the discourse of sexology introduced a new classification category, "sexual orientation." Social actors who previously were functionalized ("sodomites") were now, increasingly, classified:

> Homosexuality appeared as one of the forms of sexuality when it was transposed from the practice of sodomy onto a kind of interior androgyny, a hermaphrodism of the soul. The sodomite had been a temporary aberration; the homosexual was now a species. (Foucault, 1981: 42)

At present, the category of "belonging to a company or organization" plays a more important role in identification (e.g., "a Warwick University scientist," "a Hambro countrywide chain spokesman").

The extent to which functionalization and classification are distinct is also historically and culturally variable. In the 1960s, sociological role theory went a long way in blurring the two types of categorization:

> Every role in society has attached to it a certain identity. As we have seen, some of these identities are trivial and temporary ones, as in some occupations that demand little modification in the being of their practitioners. It is not difficult to change from garbage collector to night watchman. It is considerably more difficult to change from negro to white. And it is almost impossible to change from man to woman. These differences in the ease of role changing ought not to blind us to the fact that

even identities we consider to be our essential selves have been socially assigned. (P. L. Berger, 1966: 115)

Psychological or psychologizing discourses, on the other hand, stress the boundaries strongly, as in this question from interviewer Caroline Jones's series of Australian Broadcasting Commission radio programs *The Search for Meaning*:

> So what would you want to say about that split we seem to have made in our habit of thinking between that which we are (our being) and how we value that; and our doing, all our performance, our work. There's a real split there, isn't there, in our society. (Jones, 1989: 136)

Do we have an identity beneath the many roles we play? Or is our identity the sum of the roles we have learned to play? My concern here is not to solve this problem, but to point out that the English language allows us to make a choice between functionalization and identification and that the use of this choice in discourse is of critical importance for discourse analysis.

That the choice has a grammatical base, a base in the language itself, can be seen from the rank order of the two types of categorization in nominal groups. Identifications can be, and frequently are, classifiers in nominal groups, functionalizations only rarely. One can, for example, say "the Asian teacher," "the homosexual musician," "the woman doctor," but not (or only in a derogatory sense) "the teacher Asian," "the musician homosexual," "the doctor woman." Only relational identifications (see below) occasionally allow functionalizations to become classifiers as, for example, in "your teacher friend." Also, classifications and physical identifications cannot be possessivated except, again, in a derogatory sense (cf. my use of "our racist"). Relational identifications, on the other hand, are almost always possessivated. But possessivation does not play the same role here as in functionalization: possessivated functionalizations signify the activation (as in "his victim") or subjection (as in "my attacker") of the possessing participant, while possessivated relational identifications signify the "belonging together," the "relationality" of the possessivated and possessing social actors (as in "my daughter" or "my mother").

Relational identification represents social actors in terms of their personal, kinship, or work relations to each other, and it is realized by a closed set of nouns denoting such relations: "friend," "aunt," "colleague," etc. Typically, they are possessivated, either by means of a possessive pronoun ("her friend") or by means of a genitive ("the child's mother") or postmodifying phrase with *of* ("a mother of five").

In contemporary Western culture, the role of relational identification has gradually become less important than that of classification and functionalization, especially where personal and kinship relations are concerned. The intrusion of such relations into the sphere of public activities may be branded as "nepotism" or "corruption" (unless you are a monarch). In other societies, however, it plays a key role. Von Sturmer (1981) has described how Australian Aborigines, when they first meet, introduce themselves primarily in terms of relational identification. They "search for relations whom they share and then establish their relationship on that basis" (1981: 13). This differs from contemporary Western introductions, where nomination and functionalization ("What do you do?") are the key to establishing a relation and where classification ("Where are you from?") comes in only when a social actor displays signs of "otherness," of differing from the social norm, for instance, a foreign accent or a dark skin. Not so among Aborigines:

MAREEBA MAN:   Where you from?
MICKEY:   I'm Edward River man. Where you from?
MAREEBA MAN:   I'm Lama Lama man. . . . do you know X?
MICKEY:   No, do you know Y?
MAREEBA MAN:   No, do you know Z?
MICKEY:   Yes, she's my auntie.
MAREEBA MAN:   That old lady is my granny. I must call you daddy.
MICKEY:   I must call you boy. You give me a cigarette. (Von Sturmer, 1981: 13)

Where kinship relations continue to be functionally important in our society, as is the case especially with the relation between mothers and children, the relevant terms become polyvalent: "mother" can be used as a functionalization ("mothering" is not the act of bringing a child into the world, but the act of giving care to a child, while "fathering" signifies only the act of begetting a child), as a nomination ("Mother . . ."), and as a relational identification ("my mother"); similarly, "child" can be a classification as well as a relational identification.

We might also note that, by the criteria developed here, terms like "lover" and "caregiver" (as synonym for "parent") introduce a measure of functionalization into the sphere of personal and kinship relations. Projections of the future, such as those in Alvin Toffler's *Futureshock* (1970), do indeed predict increasing functionalization, for example, the institutionalization of "professional families," couples bringing up other people's children for money, while the actual parents devote themselves to their careers.

Physical identification represents social actors in terms of physical characteristics which uniquely identify them in a given context. It can be realized by nouns denoting physical characteristics ("blonde," "redhead," "cripple," and so on) or by adjectives ("bearded," "tall") or by prepositional phrases with *with* or *without* postmodifying highly generalized classifications such as "man" or "woman."

2.45 A little girl with a long, fair pigtail came and stood next to Mary Kate.
2.46 "What are you doing there?" shouted the man with the large mustache.

Physical identification occurs a good deal in stories, sometimes only when a character is introduced, as in 2.45, sometimes throughout, as in the story from which 2.46 is taken. It provides social actors with a unique identity in the temporary or permanent absence of nomination, and does so by means of a salient detail. But it also, and at the same time, focuses the reader or listener on the social actor's physical characteristics, and this may be done selectively, for instance, on the basis of age or gender, as in these examples from the (Australian) *Daily Mirror*: "stunning blonde singer Toby Bishop," "chubby-cheeked Laura Vezey, 2."

In contrast to nomination, physical identification is always overdetermined (see section 12): physical attributes tend to have connotations, and these can be used to obliquely classify or functionalize social actors. "Large mustaches," for example (see example 2.46), derive, perhaps, from the mustaches of Prussian army officers, connoting a sense of rigid disciplinarianism, not only in armies and schools, but also in other contexts. The borderline between physical identification and classification is therefore far from clear-cut, as is obvious from the use of skin color for classification, or from the connotations that cling to such representations of women as "blonde" or "redhead." However, even when used for the purposes of classification, the category of physical identification remains distinct, because of its obliqueness, its overdetermination, and its apparent "empirical" innocence.

Finally, social actors can be referred to in interpersonal, rather than experiential terms. For these instances, I use the term *appraisement*: social actors are appraised when they are referred to in terms which evaluate them as good or bad, loved or hated, admired or pitied. This is realized by the set of nouns and idioms that denote such appraisement (and only such appraisement) as, for instance "the darling," "the bastard," "the wretch," or "thugs" in

2.47 [Eighty] young white thugs attacked African street vendors.

It would appear, incidentally, that negative appraisements are more plentiful than positive ones, especially in some registers, such as that spoken by Miles Davis in his ghostwritten autobiography:

2.48 I told the motherfucker as he was going out of the door "I told you not to go there stupid." (Davis, 1990: 13)

As can be expected, the "Race Odyssey" text does not categorize the individuals and groups it represents to the same degree. "Racists" and "immigrants" are categorized a good deal more than are "we," Australians. And when "we" are categorized, it is in terms of our shared national identity ("Australians"); the single instance of functionalization is "critics."

"Racists" are classified by provenance and ethnicity ("Japanese," "native Vancouverites," etc.) and in one case by age and race (the case of the "young white thugs"). "Immigrants" are classified by provenance or ethnicity in 50 percent of cases, by race ("dark-skinned," "black") in 13 percent of cases, by education or skilledness in 10 percent of cases, and once each by wealth ("poor") and religion ("Muslim"). By and large, their treatment in the representation is not all that different from that of the "racists." "Racists" and "immigrants" are also the only categories of social actor that are occasionally represented in terms of relational identity. Both constitute, in this discourse, the main "others" for "us," Australians, and therefore also the main object of classification.

High-status social actors, on the other hand, such as "government" and "experts," are always functionalized. The few instances of functionalization of "racists" and "immigrants" also concern high-status persons, such as the "mayor of Kawaguchi" and the Peruvian presidential candidate. It is a pattern which, I would think, is by no means specific to this text.

## 11. Personalization and Impersonalization

So far, I have discussed representational choices which *personalize* social actors, represent them as human beings, as realized by personal or possessive pronouns, proper names, or nouns (and sometimes adjectives as, for example, in "maternal care") whose meaning includes the feature "human." But social actors can also be *impersonalized*, represented by other means, for instance, by abstract nouns or by concrete nouns whose meanings do not include the semantic feature "human." I will distinguish two types of impersonalization: *abstraction* and *objectivation*. Abstraction occurs when social actors are represented by means of a quality assigned to them by and in the representation. One example is the way in which "poor, black, unskilled, Muslim, or illegal" immigrants are referred to by means of the term "problems" in 2.49: they are being assigned the quality of being problematic, and this quality is then used to denote them. Another example is the substitution of "the changing face of Australia" for "the new immigrants" in 2.50:

> 2.49  Australia is in danger of saddling itself up with a lot of unwanted problems.
> 2.50  Many Australians...were "bewildered" by the changing face of Australia.

Objectivation occurs when social actors are represented by means of reference to a place or thing closely associated either with their person or with the action in which they are represented as being engaged. In other words, objectivation is realized by metonymical reference. A number of types of objectivation are particularly common: *spatialization, utterance autonomization, instrumentalization*, and *somatization*.

*Spatialization* is a form of objectivation in which social actors are represented by means of reference to a place with which they are, in the given context, closely associated. This happens, for instance, when "Australians" are substituted by "Australia," as in 2.51:

> 2.51  Australia was bringing in about 70,000 migrants a year.

*Utterance autonomization* is a form of objectivation in which social actors are represented by means of reference to their utterances. This is the case, for instance, with "the report" and "surveys" in 2.52, and because it lends a kind of impersonal authority to the utterances, it is often used in connection with the utterances of high-status and "official" spokespeople:

> 2.52  This concern, the report noted, was reflected in surveys which showed that the level of support for stopping immigration altogether was at a post-war high.

*Instrumentalization* is a form of objectivation in which social actors are represented by means of reference to the instrument with which they carry out the action in which they are represented as being engaged:

> 2.53  A 120mm mortar shell slammed into Sarajevo's marketplace.

*Somatization*, finally, is a form of objectivation in which social actors are represented by means of reference to a part of their body, as in expressions such as "a safe pair of hands," or as in

2.54  She put her hand on Mary Kate's shoulder.

The noun denoting the body part is almost always premodified by a possessive pronoun or genitive referring to the "owner" of the body part, and perhaps we should, in such cases, speak of "semi-objectivation." Nevertheless, possessivated somatization still adds a touch of alienation, of Mary Kate not being involved herself: not Mary Kate, but Mary Kate's *body* is being touched, in a (possibly) unwanted and intimidating intrusion.

More generally, impersonalization can have one or more of the following effects: it can background the identity and/or role of social actors; it can lend impersonal authority or force to an action or quality of a social actor; and it can add positive or negative connotations to an action or utterance of a social actor. When, for instance, "Australia" is activated in relation to the action of "bringing in migrants" (example 2.53), the text does not tell the reader who is responsible for the action, just as in the case of nominalizations and passive agent deletions. For this reason, impersonalization abounds in the language of bureaucracy, a form of organization of human action which is governed by impersonal procedures. Abstractions, finally, add connotative meanings: the qualities abstracted from their bearers serve, in part, to interpret and evaluate them.

The "Race Odyssey" text impersonalizes "immigrants" often (eighteen times), most of the other categories of social actor only rarely: "racists" are impersonalized once, "us, Australians" three times, the "government" once, and "experts" twice. The writer of the article, on the other hand, impersonalizes himself every time he refers to his actions ("italicizing," "highlighting," "calling into question," etc.), and the only personalized reference to him is the byline ("David Jenkins argues...").

Most of the impersonalizations of "immigrants" are abstractions (83 percent) and what is abstracted is, in eight out of fifteen cases, quantity: "immigrants" are referred to as "levels," "settings," etc. The qualities of being "problematic" (see 2.51), of "changing Australia" (2.52), and of "race" (as in "racial tolerance") account for the other cases.

Utterance autonomization occurs in relation to "experts" and also in relation to the writer of the article, who represents himself every single time as though, through his person, "the facts speak for themselves," as realized by the substitution of anaphoric reference to preceding sections of text for reference to his person:

2.55  They [these developments] highlight the fact that racism is seldom far below the surface.

## 12. Overdetermination

*Overdetermination* occurs when social actors are represented as participating, at the same time, in more than one social practice. One of the children's stories I analyzed,

a Dutch story called "De Metro van Magnus" (Van Leeuwen, 1981), features a character called "the Unknown Soldier." Magnus, the hero of the story, finds the Unknown
Soldier (who is "maybe 18 years old" but "looks more like a boy than like a man")
in the Unknown Soldier Square, where he sits, rather forlorn, at the foot of a huge
abstract monument dedicated to the Unknown Soldier. As this monument bears little
resemblance to a soldier, Magnus assumes that the "man-boy" must be the Unknown
Soldier. The latter, after some hesitation, agrees. He is glad to get a name, because he
himself does not know who he is (he is "unknown"). Magnus and the Unknown Soldier then go to a place "rather like a school" where the Unknown Soldier fails miserably at answering the questions asked by "the man with the large mustache" (already
featured in example 2.46). Thus the Unknown Soldier is connected to at least two
social practices, warfare and schooling, and comes to symbolize the subjected participant in both of these practices and, indeed, in all practices that produce victims
and underdogs. Magnus's own name is also overdetermined, since he is both little, a
child, and "magnus": through this name, he transcends the difference between "what
adults (can) do" and "what children (can) do."

I have distinguished four major categories of overdetermination: *inversion, symbolization, connotation*, and *distillation*.

*Inversion* is a form of overdetermination in which social actors are connected
to two practices which are, in a sense, each other's opposites. This happens, for
instance, in the well-known comic strip *The Flintstones* and other similar comics,
such as *Hagar the Horrible*. The activities of the Flintstones are very much those of
a twentieth-century American suburban family. The Flintstones themselves, however, are overdetermined: they *do* things that twentieth-century families do, but they
*look like*, and are nominated as, prehistoric cave dwellers. In other words, they have
been transformed from +contemporary to –contemporary—while still involved in
contemporary activities. Reference thus broadens to include prehistoric as well as
contemporary practices, perhaps in order that the latter may be viewed as "natural,"
as transcending history and culture: overdetermination is one of the ways in which
texts can legitimize practices. The "Magnus" example above is also a case of inversion: Magnus has been transformed from +child to –child while still involved in
childlike activities.

*Symbolization*, as I use the term here, occurs when a "fictional" social actor or
group of social actors stands for actors or groups in nonfictional social practices.
The "fictional" actor often belongs to a mythical, distant past. This distance then
allows the actors and the activities in which they engage to refer to several nonfictional actors and practices. Will Wright (1975), in a study of the western film
genre, has shown how the participants and actions in westerns changed in the early
1960s toward a pattern which he calls the "professional plot." Characteristic of this
kind of plot is the transition from individualization (the lone gunfighter who arrives
in town on his horse) to collectivization, the team of fiercely independent men who
work for money rather than for love, justice, or honor; are technically competent
and highly organized; and form a tightly knit elite with a strong code of solidarity
within the group. Wright then shows how these "professional heroes" and their
exploits can be linked to a number of social practices and the social actors involved
in them, noting, for instance, how in business the individual entrepreneur has

made way for the executive team, in science the individual genius for the efficient research team, and so on, and how the values of such teams are very similar to the values of the heroes of "professional westerns": here, too, one finds high technical competence, work for financial rewards, group solidarity against outsiders, and so on. Thus the "professional heroes" in westerns can stand for a variety of actors in actual social practices: doctors, scientists, politicians, business executives, etc. The township, the "weak society" for which the "professional heroes" work and which they are charged to protect, can stand for such social actors as the doctor's patients, the corporation's consumers, the politician's voters, etc. In other words, the social actors, and, indeed, the other elements of "professional westerns" are overdetermined. Bruno Bettelheim (1979) has similarly mapped the social actors and actions in fairy tales on to contemporary and actual social practices, notably those of the modern middle-class family.

*Connotation* occurs when a unique determination (a nomination or physical identification) stands for a classification or functionalization. This definition essentially accords with the way Barthes (1967, 1970, 1977) defined "myth" or "connotation." Connotations, says Barthes (1977: 50) are "discontinuous," "scattered traits," the knowledge of which is established by cultural tradition:

> A "historical grammar" of iconographic connotation ought thus to look for its material in painting, theatre, associations of ideas, stock metaphors, that is, precisely, in "culture." (Barthes, 1977: 22)

We have already come across an example when we discussed the case of the "man with the large mustache" (example 2.46): the reader's knowledge of popular culture associates such mustaches with the Prussian military, and then projects into the "man with the large mustache" all of the qualities which the popular culture tradition associates with the Prussian military. Such knowledge is not necessarily conscious. It is "mythical" knowledge. The signs "are not understandable, but merely reminiscent of cultural lessons half-learnt" (J. Berger, 1972: 140)—perhaps most frequently from the mass media, movies, comic strips, and so on.

*Distillation* realizes overdetermination through a combination of generalization and abstraction. It is perhaps best explained by means of an example. A section of a chapter from Ivan Illich's *Deschooling Society* (1973), which I have analyzed in some detail elsewhere (Van Leeuwen, 1993b), establishes, in the course of the text, the taxonomy displayed in table 2.3.

Three observations can be made about this taxonomy. First, while "psychiatrist," and perhaps also "guidance counselor," can be seen as true hyponyms of "therapist," "schoolteachers," "ministers," "job counselors," and "lawyers" are not usually classified as therapists. They may adopt some of the values and manners of therapists, but therapy is not the central aspect of their activities. In other words, Illich has abstracted what would normally be regarded as relatively peripheral qualities and then elevated them to the status of generalizations. This is borne out by the way he formulates the superordinate term: "professional" can be regarded as a true generalization of "schoolteachers," "ministers," etc., and it is this term which is used as head of the nominal group.

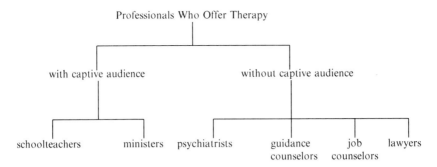

TABLE 2.3. Distillation Taxonomy

Second, "therapy" features only in the qualifier of the nominal group. The term cannot, by itself, be used to refer to teachers. In other formulations, Illich uses "therapist" as circumstance of role ("the teacher-as-therapist"); again, therapist is a circumstantial rather than a central feature. The same can be said for "with captive audience" and "without captive audience": in relation to "schoolteacher," "minister," etc., this is circumstantial, and hence an abstraction rather than a generalization. One cannot say that schoolteachers are a kind of therapist "with captive audience."

Third, and most important in the present context, the taxonomy is not exhaustive. It is not constructed in order to chart the field of therapy, but in order to delegitimize the actions of teachers by means of a comparison (the intrusion of fields other than those that form the main topic of a text for the sake of comparison always has a legitimizing or delegitimizing function). Illich compares the actions of schoolteachers to the actions of ministers and priests. The church is an institution which, in the eyes of the "radical" readers Illich was addressing when he wrote this book in the 1960s, had already been delegitimized long ago. The delegitimation of schools, on the other hand, was, and still is, a more controversial matter. Through overdetermining teachers, through connecting them to both school and church, some of the already achieved delegitimation of the church can be transferred to the school, to teachers, and to their actions: "Children are protected by neither the First, nor the Fifth amendment when they stand before that secular priest, the teacher" (Illich, 1973: 38).

Distillation, then, is a form of overdetermination which connects social actors to several social practices by abstracting the same feature from the social actors involved in these several practices.

Finally, I shall briefly discuss the two most common forms of *inversion*: *anachronism* and *deviation*. Of the former, we have already encountered an example, that of the Flintstones; science fiction can provide another example. Here, social actors are projected into the future (and perhaps onto another planet as well)—but their actions often bear a remarkable resemblance to contemporary practices. Anachronism is often used to say things that cannot be said straightforwardly, for instance, to offer social and political criticism in circumstances where this is proscribed by official or commercial censorship, or to naturalize ideological discourses.

In the case of deviation, social actors involved in certain activities are represented by means of reference to social actors who would not normally be eligible to engage in these activities. In children's stories about the first day at school, for instance, reference to children might be replaced by reference to animals, a transformation of the feature +human into −human:

2.56  The teacher wrote the name down in the register: NOIL.
Then she finished calling the register.
"Betty Small," she said.
"Yes," said the little girl.
"Noil," said the teacher.
"Yes," said the lion. He sat next to the little girl, as good as gold.

This overdetermination fuses "what children (can) do" and "what animals (can) do" and so causes the child to be represented as, at the same time, human and animal, "civilized" and "uncivilized," and also as at the same time weak ("small," "little") and strong. The deviation lies in the transgression of the rule that animals cannot go to school: more naturalistic stories about the first day at school invariably include the episode of the dog who wants to come to school too, but is not allowed to, and then feels sad and abandoned, while the child does not, or at least not initially, understand why his or her dog may not come to school. When, in a fantasy story like the one quoted in 2.56, animals transgress the eligibility rule and do go to school, they must necessarily fail. In the case of Noil, the lion, this does not happen, however, until after Noil has scared off the boy who teases Betty Small in the playground.

Deviation almost always serves the purpose of legitimation: the failure of the deviant social actor confirms the norms. In the case of Noil and Betty Small, it justifies the eligibility rule and so legitimizes school as the necessary transition from a state of being in which children "are at one with the animal" to a state of being in which they "rise above animals," a state of being in which, paradoxically, they are represented as "small," "little," and timid, rather than as confident and assertive in their new status.

The "Race Odyssey" text features only one overdetermination, the title, which overdetermines a process, rather than the social actors involved in it, the process of "coming home after a long journey," of finding "our" ("racial") identity, and which, of course, is also a headline-style pun on the Kubrick movie 2001: A Space Odyssey.. If I had chosen to exemplify my account of the representation of the social actors involved in the immigration process with a fictional example, I would probably have had a greater number of instances of overdetermination to discuss.

## 13.  Conclusion

Table 2.4 summarizes, in the form of a system network, my answer to the question with which I started: what are the principal ways in which social actors can be represented in discourse? The square brackets in the diagram stand for either-or choices (e.g., social actors must be either "activated" or "passivated"), the curly brackets stand for simultaneous choices (e.g., social actors can be both "activated" and "personalized," and so on). I hope that my discussion of the various categories in

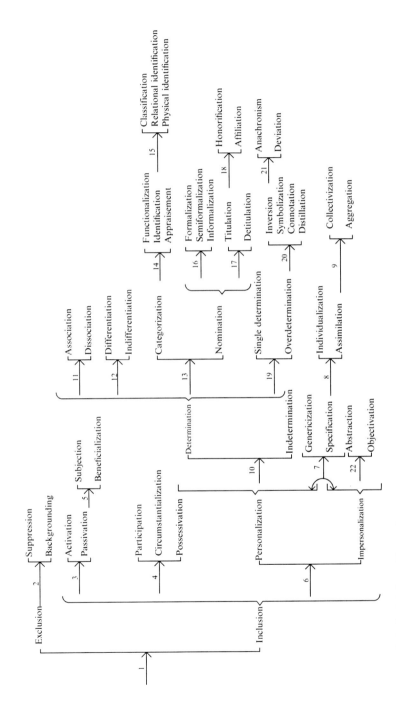

TABLE 2.4. Social Actor Network

52

the network has made it clear that, in actual discursive practices, the choices need not always be rigidly either-or. Boundaries can be blurred deliberately, for the purpose of achieving specific representational effects, and social actors can be, for instance, both classified and functionalized. In such cases, the categories remain nevertheless distinct and useful for making explicit how the social actors are represented.

The network brings together what linguists tend to keep separate: it involves a number of distinct lexicogrammatical and discourse-level linguistic systems, transitivity, reference, the nominal group, rhetorical figures, and so on, because all of these systems are involved in the realization of representations of social actors. Nevertheless, there is some linguistic consistency in the network. Initially, it involves three of the major types of transformation: deletion (systems 1 and 2), rearrangement (systems 3–5), and substitution (systems 6–22). Each type of transformation involves distinct linguistic systems: deletion involves voice, and also nominalization and adjectivalization; rearrangement principally involves transitivity; while substitution is initially realized by aspects of the structure of the nominal group—the deictic and the postdeictic, that is, the system of reference (systems 7, 8, 10, and 12) and the numerative (system 9; cf. Halliday, 1985, ch. 6; Matthiessen, 1992, ch. 3.2)—and then by lexis, different classes of noun, including aspects of morphological structure (systems 13–18). Systems 19–22, finally, involve various forms of metaphor and metonym. More globally, the three sections 7–12, 13–18, and 19–22 involve, respectively, reference, lexis (the field of nouns referring to human beings), and metaphor.

I will, finally, summarize my discussion of the "Race Odyssey" text, which, of course, has restricted itself to the representation of social actors and therefore not dealt with many other salient and critically relevant features of this text.

Those who, in some way or other, are represented as being "concerned about" or actually opposing immigration and immigrants in countries other than Australia, I have referred to as "racists": in the article, they are unfavorably compared to opponents of ("high") migration in Australia, who have "reasonable" rather than "racist" concerns about immigration. As we have seen, representation of these "racists" is relatively often suppressed or backgrounded. This has to be offset against the fact that the exclusions follow very definite categorizations, such as "80 young white thugs." It can be argued that the article invites us to interpret these vague or missing representations in the light of this initial categorization, which has no equivalent in the representation of Australian opponents of immigration. "Racists" are also often referred to generically. And they are individualized and nominated only when elite persons are concerned. On the other hand, they are frequently activated in relation to (passivated) immigrants, and this with respect to both material and verbal processes, such as "denying entry" and "insulting," and mental processes, such as "being concerned." When they are classified, they are most frequently classified in much the same way as are immigrants, by "where they are from," so that they have at least this in common with those other undesirables, the immigrants themselves. Negative appraisement, finally, occurs in connection with this category of social actors, and it occurs the very first time they are referred to (again, the case of the "80 young white thugs").

Bruce Roxton, the homegrown "racist," is represented as equally undesirable. But, unlike "racists" abroad, he is never backgrounded, and he is individualized as well as nominated. Like other "racists," he is highly activated in relation to (passive) immigrants. In other words, at home, one can easily single out the few deviant individuals who, unlike "us," Australians, deserve the epithet "racist," and then turn them into the notorious personifications of prejudice and bigotry which "we" all (and especially the media) love to hate. Abroad, on the other hand, racism is much more pervasive.

Another group of social actors who oppose or worry about immigrants and immigration is formed by "us," the Australian people "as a whole." This group is more sympathetically treated—less often backgrounded, less often referred to generically, and classified, if at all, only as "Australians." If they are activated, it is in relation to mental processes, such as being "bewildered" and "not understanding," "feeling unable to cope," and so on, rather than in relation to material and verbal processes, as in the case of the "racists." And finally, they form a collective, which underlines their supposed consensus about immigration issues.

The immigrants themselves I have referred to as "them," and "they" are relatively often backgrounded and often referred to generically, which helps to distance the reader from them. They are either assimilated or aggregated, and the aggregations help to represent them as a large "horde" about to invade "us," and as the object of "rational" calculation, rather than as fellow human beings. They are also represented abstractly, and this, again, frequently involves the abstraction of their number. More than any other category of social actors, they are classified by their "ethnic origin," class, race, level of education, wealth, and so on—differences which are not made in relation to "us," Australians. And immigrants from different ethnic origins are sometimes lumped together in what I have called "associations," to create further categories of migrant. If they are activated, finally, it is almost always in relation to one activity, that of "immigrating": in every other respect, they are acted *upon* by others.

The government is rarely backgrounded or referred to generically, and it is often individualized and nominated, that is, personified in the person of the prime minister. It also transcends classification and is always functionalized and playing a highly active role in relation to the immigrants. The social actors who form the executive arm of the government, however, those who must actually "stop" the immigrants, are suppressed: the article keeps the reality of "cutting back immigration" at a comfortable distance from the reader.

"Experts" are represented in two ways. Either they are treated like elite persons (highly activated, functionalized, individualized, nominated, and titulated), or their utterances are autonomized and/or collectivized, to imbue them with impersonal authority and a sense of consensus among experts.

The writer of the article also refers to himself and to his readers. The latter are addressed directly, the former makes "the facts" speak in his stead. It is not the author himself, for instance, but "they" (i.e., "these developments") which "highlight the fact that racism is seldom far below the surface." Whether or not the writer is also the social actor who legitimizes the "fears" of "us," Australians, and "entitles" "us" (and Prime Minister Hawke) to our feelings of pride, concern, etc., is not clear. Although this legitimizing social actor plays an important role in the process of immigration, reference to him or her is always suppressed. Perhaps we are not too far from the truth as we recognize here, through traces in the text itself, the highly active role of the media in this social process, despite the careful stance of neutrality suggested by the way in which most of the representation is attributed to sources other than the writer himself.

# 3

# Representing Social Action

$\mathbf{I}$n this chapter, originally written as a companion paper to the paper on which chapter 2 is based, I continue the analysis of the "Race Odyssey" text, focusing, this time, on social actions rather than on social actors, and asking the question "What are the ways in which social action can be represented in English discourse?"

## 1. Introduction

Even a short quote can bring out the critical relevance of analyzing the representation of social action:

> 3.1 Many Australians, the 1988 Fitzgerald Committee reported, were "bewildered" by the changing face of Australia today. They did not feel they understood or could influence this change. They felt "besieged" by immigration.

Three kinds of social action are represented here: the action of "immigrating," the reactions of "many Australians" to this action, and the "reporting" of these reactions by "the 1988 Fitzgerald Committee." But they are not represented in the same way. The "reporting" of the committee and the reactions of Australians are represented as the doings and feelings of specific social actors, as observable and tangible occurrences. "Immigration," on the other hand, is objectivated, represented as a generalized and intangible "phenomenon" rather than as an action by specific social actors and as the equally intangible, yet inescapable quasi-natural process of "change." At the same time, it is also represented as affecting the Australian people, as "bewildering" and "besieging" them. Thus immigration itself remains an unexamined and unexaminable given, while the reactions to it are represented in all of their specifics, as though they should be our main focus of attention.

Representational choices such as these play a key role in the "Race Odyssey" text. They form part of a particular kind of racist discourse, a discourse based on fear—fear of loss of livelihood and loss of cultural identity, fear of the unknown and unknowable "other." But they also have very precise grammatical and rhetorical realizations: the reactions of Australians are represented through active verbs ("they felt..."); the actions of immigrants through nominalizations ("immigration"); the reports of the committee are represented through specific speech act verbs ("the 1988 Fitzgerald Committee reported..."); and the actions of immigrants are represented through abstractions ("change") and metaphors ("besiege"). In this chapter, I will bring these two elements together. I will present a descriptive framework for critically analyzing modes of representing social action, using critical, sociosemantic categories such as "objectivation," "naturalization," etc., but relating them to the specific grammatical and rhetorical realizations which can help to identify them in texts. In short, I am sketching the outline of a sociological "grammar" of the representation of social action—a systematic inventory of the ways in which action can be represented in English and their import in discourse.

## 2. Reactions

The government officials, experts, "concerned citizens," immigrants, and others featured in the "Race Odyssey" text are represented as involved, not only in actions, but also in *reactions*. They have "legitimate fears" about immigration, feel "bewildered" and "besieged," express "concerns," and so on, and the question of who is represented as reacting how to whom, or what, can be a revealing diagnostic for critical discourse analysis. My corpus of "first day at school" texts contains many reactions. Children's stories, for instance, not only try to make children comply with the rules of school but also, and above all, to *like* school, to feel happy in school. Texts aimed at parents, similarly, show parents not only what to do, but also what to feel ("don't worry if your child cries," "enjoy the time you now have to yourself," and so on).

Sociological role theory recognizes this distinction. A role is not merely "a regulatory pattern for externally visible actions," it also carries with it "the emotions and attitudes that belong to these actions" (Berger, 1966: 113). Role theorists see this as resulting more or less directly from performing the actions and leave the question of power out of consideration. Berger cites the case of the military officer: "With every salute given and accepted, our man is fortified in his new bearing....He not only acts like an officer, he feels like one" (1966: 114). The children in "first day" texts, on the other hand, are subjected to power, and the texts reflect an underlying concern about whether they will emotionally identify with their new role and with the institution in which it is played out. Texts such as these do not attribute reactions equally to all participants. Children's books dwell on the reactions of children, not on those of parents and teachers. Texts addressing parents dwell on the reactions of parents and children, not on those of teachers, and so on. As the power of social actors decreases, the amount of emotive reactions attributed to them increases.

REPRESENTING SOCIAL ACTION    57

How are reactions grammatically distinct from actions? Halliday's transitivity theory (1967–1968, 1985) provides some clear criteria: "mental processes" are, in English, distinct from the processes that realize actions ("material," "behavioral," and "verbal" processes) in four ways. First, unlike material, behavioral, and verbal processes, they cannot be "probed" by means of a "do" question (one can answer the question "What was he doing?" with "He was washing up," but not with "He knew that she was coming"). Second, while material, behavioral, and verbal processes take the progressive present, mental processes take the simple present (thus "I am thinking" would be an action, "I think of you" a reaction; some reactions can have behavioral manifestations). Third, the "senser" of a mental process (the participant whose mental process it is, who thinks, fears, desires, etc.) must be human or, more precisely, is treated as capable of human mental processes by the very fact of being "senser" in a mental process: pets may be represented as "sensers," for instance. Finally, the "phenomenon" (the object of the mental process, that which is thought, feared, desired, etc.) can be realized by a clause as well as by a nominal group (one can say "I knew he was coming" as well as "I knew him," for instance).

However, these criteria are not always sufficient for the identification of actions and reactions in actual texts, because they are bound up with the grammar of the clause, and fail to provide recognition criteria for actions and reactions realized at other linguistic levels, for instance, by elements of the nominal group, as with "unwanted" in example 3.2 and "tolerance" in example 3.3, or across two clauses, as in example 3.4:

3.2 Australia is...in danger of saddling itself with a lot of unwanted problems.
3.3 Racial tolerance is wearing thin.
3.4 They were just a little nervous. Would the teacher be strict?

Also, many reactions are not realized dynamically, by "mental process" clauses such as "they feared...," but statically, by descriptive clauses such as "they were afraid..." In other words, the *grammatical* category "mental process" does not fully overlap with the sociosemantic category "reaction." As already discussed in the previous chapter, Halliday deals with this problem through his theory of grammatical metaphor (1985: ch. 10): the sociosemantic concept "mental process" is said to be realized literally (or "congruently") when it is realized by the grammatical category "mental process" and metaphorically when it is realized in other ways, for instance, by a static descriptive clause. Thus, "I fear you" would be literal, "I am afraid of you" metaphorical. The two are different, of course, but I would prefer not to privilege one over the other as somehow more congruent with reality, or otherwise more basic. They are two different ways of representing reactions, embodying two different views of what reactions are, both equally metaphorical or equally literal: "Metaphors are not things to be seen beyond. One can see beyond them only by using other metaphors" (Lakoff and Johnson, 1980: 239). The point is to inventorize the different metaphors available for representing reaction, insofar as they are critically nontrivial and can be coupled with distinct lexicogrammatical realizations.

Reactions can be *unspecified*, through verbs like "react" and "respond" and their related nouns, adjectives, and adverbs, or *specified* as particular types of reaction, and to trace which types of reaction are, in a given discourse, attributed to which social actors can, again, be revealing. Some discourses, for example, in the field of advertising, represent the behavior of the "consumer" (the "voter," the "audience," etc.) as predominantly motivated by affective reactions, by desires, needs, and wants. The reactions which advertisers, planners of campaigns, etc., attribute to themselves, on the other hand, are more likely to be cognitive and rational: again, the greater the power of social actors, the more likely it is that cognitive, rather than affective, reactions will be attributed to them.

Halliday distinguishes three types of reaction, again on the basis of grammatical criteria. In contrast to *cognitive* and *perceptive* mental processes, *affective* mental processes can take "proposals" as their object, that is, they can combine with perfective nonfinite clauses with "to," as in example 3.5, and infinitive or imperfective nonfinite clauses with the -*ing* participle, as in example 3.6 (cf. Halliday, 1985: 235ff.):

3.5  A number of critics want to see our intake halved to 70,000 to 80,000.

3.6  Mary Kate liked being the last name on the register.

Perceptive mental processes are distinct in being able to take another kind of nonfinite construction, the "accusative cum infinitivo," as in 3.7, or its "progressive" version, as in 3.8 (cf. Matthiessen, 1992: 108):

3.7  I heard him walk away.

3.8  I heard him walking away.

Cognitive mental processes can take "propositions" as their object, "that" clauses (in which "that" may be elided), as in 3.9 (cf. Halliday, 1985: 235ff.):

3.9  He [the prime minister] thinks our current intake is about right.

Finally, certain key perceptive verbs, such as "see" and "perceive," and certain affective verbs, such as "feel" and "fear," can act as cognitive processes and take "propositions" as their object, as in 3.10:

3.10  They did not feel they understood or could influence this change.

This introduces a different interpretation of the cognitive process, and a different grounding for the knowledge expressed, lending it a perceptive flavor, in which "seeing" becomes like "knowing," or an affective flavor, in which the difference between "feeling" and "thinking" is diminished, so that "feelings" can support "propositions." Other dimensions of the representation of reactions, such as the difference between "I fear..." and "I am afraid..." (between what, below, will be called "activation" and "descriptivization"), can also apply to actions and will be discussed in later sections.

Applying this framework to an analysis of the "Race Odyssey" text, we can observe, first of all, that the text contains 113 representations of actions (73 percent) and 42 representations of reactions (27 percent): reactions clearly play a significant role in the way immigration is represented here. The vast majority of these reactions is attributed to "Australians" (52 percent) and their government (21 percent) and to those who are "concerned about" or "resentful of" immigrants in other countries (19 percent). The reactions of immigrants, on the other hand, are not represented. Immigrants only *provoke* reactions. Their thoughts and feelings and observations are not considered relevant. The text is squarely written from the point of view of those who have, or aspire to have, the power to regulate the "intake" of migrants, to "cut" it, "halve" it, and so on—even though the text also tells us that 40 percent of Australians were either born overseas or have at least one parent who was.

There is a distinct pattern also in the distribution of the different *types* of reactions. Anti-immigration reactions in countries other than Australia are for the most part affective, emotional, unreasonable. Anti-immigration reactions within Australia, on the other hand, are as often cognitive ("believe," "consider," "think," etc.) as affective (although some of the cognitive reactions have an affective "flavor"): the "legitimate fears" of Australians are not portrayed as irrational fears, but as *reasonable* fears, emotions checked and held in balance by rational considerations, this in contrast to the emotions of the true "racists" in other countries. "Resentment" is reserved for Bruce Roxton, the racist the Australian media love to hate, as the exception to the rule that Australians are not racist and have only reasonable and understandable "concerns" about immigration. The Australian government's reactions, finally, are for the most part cognitive, and the affective reactions attributed to it are positive ("hope, "be disposed to"), this despite the fact that the article criticizes the government's immigration policy and in keeping with the general pattern in the media that "emotiveness" decreases as status and power increase.

## 3. Material and Semiotic Action

Social action can be interpreted as *material* or *semiotic*, as "doing" or as "meaning," in other words, as action which has, at least potentially, a material purpose or effect or as action which does not. Examples 3.11 and 3.12, for instance, represent the same stage in the "first day" scenario, the child's rebellion against entering school for the first time, but where 3.11 "materializes" it, 3.12 "semioticizes" it:

3.11  Darren resisted the teacher's attempts to settle him.
3.12  "We don't want to sit down," said Magnus. "We want to go outside."

The same contrast can be observed in these two versions of a speech act by Nelson Mandela, both from the *Times* (7 February 1994): in 3.13, it is materialized, represented as action ("attacks"), in 3.14 semioticized, represented as meaning ("described"):

3.13  The ruling National Party has urged Mr. Mandela to end his attacks on President de Klerk.
3.14  Mr. Mandela described the President as a weakling who had not raised a word of protest against right-wing attacks on ANC offices and cared nothing for black lives.

Again, the point is not that one is metaphorical and the other literal, but that the same action is represented in two different ways, each conveying a distinct attitude toward, and interpretation of, the action; the one equating the power of words and deeds, the other distinguishing between the semiotic act of "describing" and the material act of "attacking ANC offices."

The distinction between material and semiotic action can be related to specific grammatical realizations (see Halliday, 1985: ch. 5). "Verbal processes" occupy an intermediate position between material and mental processes, between actions and reactions. On the one hand, they resemble doings (one can answer the question "What did she do?" with "She is saying her prayers"). On the other hand, they resemble cognitive mental processes, in that they can take a "proposition" as their object, which is not the case with material processes (one cannot say "Mr. Mandela attacked that the president was a weakling").

Material actions can be transactive or nontransactive. The former involve two participants, the "actor," the "one who does the deed," and the "goal," "the one to which the process is extended" (Halliday, 1985: 102–5). The goal, according to Halliday, must be a "thing," that is, "a phenomenon of our experience, including, of course, our inner experience or imagination—some entity (person, creature, object, institution or abstraction); or some process (action, event, quality, state or relation)" (1985: 108). Nontransactive actions involve only one participant, the "actor," who in the case of "behavioral processes," must be human. This distinction is not just a neutral, grammatical one. It distinguishes also between actions which have an effect on others, or on the world, and actions which do not. In "first day" texts, for instance, children's actions are mostly nontransactive: children are rarely represented as having an effect on the world. They may play, run around, whine, cry, draw, or sing, but who they are running to or playing with, what their whining and crying achieves, or what it is they draw or sing about, is not represented, at least not in "first day" texts aimed at adults. Children's actions are portrayed here as mere behavior, without content, purpose, or effect, and this is not so in the case of teachers, whose actions are almost invariably represented as affecting the children in their care. The actions of migrants in the "Race Odyssey" text also tend to be nontransactive: they "immigrate," "arrive," constitute a "mere trickle" or "an influx," and so on. Clearly, the ability to "transact" requires a certain power, and the greater that power, the greater the range of "goals" that may be affected by an actor's actions.

Halliday's description of the "goal" of a material process is very broad, and it may be critically relevant to distinguish between transactions with things and transactions with people. Grammatically, "material processes" may treat both as "things." Critically, it is important to distinguish between actions which affect people and actions which affect other kinds of "things." I will refer to the former as *interactive* and to the latter as *instrumental* transactions. In the case of interaction, the action is referred to by means of a verb which can only take a human goal, as with "hug" in 3.15 and "deny entry" in 3.16; if the goals of such verbs are not human, they can usually be interpreted as metonymical displacements (as when someone "kisses the ground" on which someone else has stood), instrumentalizations of social actors (e.g., in expressions like "the bullet killed him"), or projections of human social practices onto the behavior of animals, plants, and even inanimate matter:

3.15  Mary Kate ran to her and hugged her.
3.16  People of Asian descent...have been denied entry to elegant restaurants.

In *instrumental* transactions, the goal may be either human or nonhuman. In other words, instrumental transactions represent people as interchangeable with objects, for instance, through verbs like "use," "transport," "destroy," "carry," etc. Not surprisingly, instrumentalizations are common in texts which are to some degree bureaucratized (as with "make use of other children" in 3.17) and less common, for instance, in stories (cf. 3.18), where the transaction might, literally and figuratively, be represented as interactive, dialogic:

3.17  Make use of other children to help him get dressed or use scissors.
3.18  "Susan," called Miss Laurie, "show Mary Kate the doll's house and all the other things."

The same distinctions apply to semiotic action. Semiotic action can be transactive (as in "she addressed him") or not (as in "she spoke for an hour"). Again, the actions of lower-status actors are more often represented as nontransactive:

3.19  When she woke up the children were singing.

The instrumentalization of semiotic transactions is realized through verbs of "exchange" and "transport," e.g., "give," "offer," "receive," "provide," "supply," "convey," "put across," usually together with some kind of specification of the kind of speech act involved (e.g., "information" in 3.20) and possibly also of the content conveyed by the semiotic action (e.g., "about new entrants," also in 3.20):

3.20  More than half of our sample schools received information about new entrants from the preschools.

But semiotic action can involve an additional dimension, the very dimension which makes it semiotic: it can convey meanings. When semiotic action is *behavioralized*, this dimension is not represented, and semiotic action is treated as similar to other forms of action, divested of its ability to reach beyond the here and now of the communication situation, its ability to represent the "then" and the "there," to remember the past and imagine the future.

When semiotic action is not behavioralized, the meanings conveyed by the semiotic action are also represented, resulting in embedded representation, representation-within-the-representation. This embedding can take a number of forms. It can take the form of the *quote*, in which case it includes not only the meanings conveyed by represented social actors but also their wordings. In texts like "Race Odyssey," this is typically reserved for high-status actors (3.21) or used to enhance the credibility of an embedded representation. When there is a choice between quoting or not quoting, quoting may imply something like "I could not have said it better myself" or "No further comment or interpretation is needed" as, perhaps, in 3.22:

3.21  "I hope that as we go on," he [Prime Minister Hawke] said recently, "that we may be able to look at higher levels of immigration."

3.22 "Native Vancouverites will be made to feel like strangers in their own city…," wrote
one reader of The Province newspaper.

Many "first day" texts are procedural, telling parents or teachers what to do on
the "first day," and when such texts include quotes, there is often an unspoken suggestion that the represented wordings should be adhered to if the semiotic action is to
be effective, as in this piece of advice to parents:

3.23 Yet by being asked specifics such as "Did you make a new friend?" or "What was
the very best thing you did today?" your child may find it easy to launch into a vivid
description of their day.

*Rendition* does not include the wording and is realized by reported speech:

3.24 The mayor of Kawaguchi has "joked" that with so many dark-skinned foreigners in
town, Japanese are having trouble seeing them at night.

The content of a semiotic action may also be conveyed in a more abbreviated
form, by specifying either the nature of the signifier (*form specification*), as with "a
modicum of information" in 3.25, or that of the signified (*topic specification*), as with
"about the first day" in 3.26:

3.25 Every school requested a modicum of information from the parents.
3.26 Parents should make a point of talking about the first day.

Topic specification is typically realized by a "circumstance of matter," a phrase with
"about," "concerning," or some similar preposition (Halliday, 1985: 142), such as
"about the first day" in example 3.26. Form specification is realized by some term
denoting a kind of speech act (e.g., "joke," "story," "lesson," "nonsense") or communicative act using some other semiotic mode (e.g., "song," "drawing," "diagram").
When not accompanied by a quote, rendition, or topic specification, it is in fact close
to behavioralization and no longer represents the meanings conveyed by the semiotic action. This often occurs in the representation of semiotic acts by lower-status
social actors, for instance, in the representations of children's talk in "first day" texts
addressed to adults.

Applying the distinctions introduced in this section to the "Race Odyssey" text
shows that the key categories of social actor featured in the text are represented as
involved in different types of action. Migrants are only twice represented as involved
in semiotic action (the Pakistanis "tell lies under the name of Allah," the Sikhs
"press for the right to have Mounties in turbans in Canada"); 94 percent of their
actions are material and almost all of these are nontransactive (86 percent): migrants
just "arrive," "immigrate," "trickle in," and so on. Yet, as already mentioned, these
actions are nevertheless also represented as having an effect on Australians and
on "concerned citizens" elsewhere, albeit in an objectivated way: what affects these
"concerned citizens" is not the migrants themselves, as identifiable and specific
actors, but "migration," a vague and intangible "phenomenon."

The Australian government, too, is mostly represented as involved in material action (87 percent), and its actions are predominantly instrumental: it "takes in," "programs," "halves," "cuts," "stops," etc. Its relation to migrants is represented, not as interaction with people, but as a calculated, mechanical operation upon people.

"We," Australians, and the "racists" in other countries are represented as involved in material and semiotic action, though somewhat more in the former (69 percent material and 31 percent semiotic in the case of Australians; 60 percent material and 40 percent semiotic in the case of the "racists" in other countries). The actions of the French, Japanese, Peruvian, and Canadian "racists," however, are not instrumental like those of the Australian government. They are actual interactions. "Racists" in other countries "attack," "deny entry," "insult," and so on. The actions of "us," Australians, on the other hand, are more abstract and rarely interactive. Sometimes, nontransactive (they "sit," "read," "debate"), at other times more or less instrumental (they "avoid problems"), they always take place at the level of "public opinion," of surveys and opinion polls, of reading newspapers and contributing to "debates"; this is in contrast to the actions of "racists" elsewhere, which are represented as actual acts of racism.

Two categories of actor involved in the "debates" are represented as only contributing semiotic actions: the "experts" whose findings are rendered by the writer, and the writer himself, who "italicizes," "highlights," and "calls into question" and who represents his own words as "facts" which teach us a "lesson." The only reference to him as a person occurs in the byline ("argues David Jenkins"), but the nature of his speech acts is represented throughout: despite his careful adherence to journalistic practices such as attributing anything that could be interpreted as opinion to named "sources," the article is not a neutral "report," but an "argument" and a "lesson."

## 4. Objectivation and Descriptivization

Actions and reactions can be *activated*, represented dynamically, or *deactivated*, represented statically, as though they were entities or qualities rather than dynamic processes.

When activated, the actions or reactions are grammatically realized in the verbal group of a non-embedded clause. When deactivated, they are realized in other ways, to be discussed below. From the point of view of a theory of representation, however, they remain representations of actions and reactions.

*Objectivated* actions are realized by nominalizations or process nouns which either function as subject or object of the clause (as with "migration from traditional source countries" in 3.27) or form part of a prepositional phrase (as with "immigration" in 3.28):

3.27 Migration from traditional source countries like Italy and Greece has dried up.
3.28 They cannot voice legitimate fears about immigration without being branded racist.

Objectivation can also be realized metonymically, by various kinds of displacement, for instance, by *temporalization*, the substitution of the time associated with an action or reaction for the action or reaction itself (as with "about the day ahead" in 3.29); by *spatialization*, the substitution of a place associated with an action or reaction for the action or reaction itself (as with "school" in 3.30); or by various forms of *prolepsis*, for instance, the substitution of the product of an action or reaction for the action or reaction itself (as with "no parting tears" in 3.31):

3.29 The family can talk calmly and happily about the day ahead.
3.30 School is just about to begin.
3.31 I saw no parting tears.

This does not exhaust the possibilities. Another form of displacement, common in "psychological" fiction, is the displacement of reactions onto the weather, as in the following quote from a detective novel by Georges Simenon (1979: 111), where the first clause objectivates the reaction of the hero, and the second the hero himself, by substituting "the rain" for the hero, as "senser" of a (descriptivized) mental process:

3.32 It was still raining the following day. The rain was soft, cheerless and hopeless, like a widow's tears.

When an action or reaction is objectivated, the representation downgrades it in order to give priority to something else. In procedural texts, for example, priority might be given to sequencing, as in 3.33, or to signaling whether an action or reaction is optional or obligatory (or something in between: "helpful," "advisable," "desirable," etc.) as in 3.34:

3.33 Preparation for the first day at school should start early.
3.34 Meeting the teacher is also important.

In texts which juxtapose several representations of the same practice, priority might be given to modality:

3.35 It would seem that it is logistically possible to include mothers in the classroom.

Very frequently, however, objectivation serves to add purposes and/or legitimations to the representation. Here is an example from Illich's *Deschooling Society* (1973: 51):

3.36 Alienation was a direct consequence of wage labour which deprived man of the opportunity to create and recreate. Now young people are pre-alienated by schools that isolate them while they pretend to be both producers and consumers of their own knowledge, which is conceived of as a commodity put on the market in school.

The first clause of this excerpt contains two objectivations: "alienation" and "wage labour." These objectivations allow the two actions ("working for a wage" and "alienating") to be linked to each other by a causal process ("was a direct consequence of"). Thus, the negative connotation of "alienation" can transfer to "working for a wage" and, by means of an implicit comparison, also to schooling, Illich's main topic. In other words, verbs denoting logical relations can link objectivated actions to each other in order to evaluate and thereby legitimize or delegitimize them. In texts like Illich's *Deschooling Society*, legitimation and delegitimation are in fact the overriding concern, and representing the social actions involved in "schooling" takes a back seat. However, legitimation and delegitimation cannot stand on their own. They must be related to a representation of the actions and reactions which they legitimate or delegitimate, however reduced, generalized, and abstract this representation may be.

Objectivation also allows social actions to be classified, labeled. The objectivated action or reaction then premodifies another objectivation which abstracts an aspect or quality from that action, for instance, its "ritual" or "formal" or "strategic" nature:

3.37 Entry procedures are largely a matter for the head teacher to decide.
3.38 Local education authorities vary in their admission policies.
3.39 Children learn most of what their teachers pretend to teach them from...mere participation in the ritual of school.

This, too, can play a role in the realization of legitimation. To call an action or set of actions a "ritual," for instance, delegitimizes it/them, bringing negative connotations of "emptiness" and "hollowness" to bear on the action of "schooling."

Actions and reactions can also be *descriptivized*, that is, they can be represented as more or less permanent qualities of social actors (as, for example, with "smiling" in example 3.40 and "specially trained" in example 3.41) or of other elements of the represented practice, e.g., the props required for its enactment, as with "her favorite video" in 3.42:

3.40 A smiling teacher met them at the door.
3.41 A specially trained squad of teachers will go into homes to show parents how to prepare their children for formal education.
3.42 A quiet way of celebrating her first day at school might be a viewing of her favorite video.

Reactions are often descriptivized in this way:

3.43 Is...this nation...impervious to racist sentiment?
3.44 We are entitled to be proud...about our immigration program.

Descriptivization can be realized by epithets, as in 3.40, 3.41, and 3.42, or by the attributes of descriptive clauses as, for instance, in 3.43 and 3.44.

In the "Race Odyssey" text, only 53 percent of actions and reactions are activated. But the amount of deactivation is not constant throughout the text. In the first twelve lines, the section which deals with the behavior of the "racists" in other countries, activation is much more frequent (74 percent). The actions and reactions of these "racists" are rarely deactivated: in 81 percent of cases, they are placed squarely in the foreground of the text. The actions of the writer of the article and of the various experts whose reports and surveys are quoted are also predominantly activated.

"We," Australians, are activated in 54 percent of cases. Objectivation occurs mostly in relation to actions and reactions that could be interpreted negatively: "fear," "disharmony," "dislocation," and so on. Descriptivizations, which represent actions or reactions as more or less permanent qualities of social actors, occur most often in relation to relatively positive reactions (see 3.43 and 3.44 above, for instance). Activation is thus used to foreground the rational and nonracist nature of Australians' concerns about immigration ("believe," "think," "feel") and to background their basis in feelings of insecurity and fear.

The actions and reactions of the Australian government are activated in 44 percent of cases, mainly in relation to semiotic actions ("say") and reactions ("think," "believe," "hope"). The government's material actions, on the other hand, the actions which materially affect migrants ("program," "cut," "stop," etc.) are objectivated, backgrounded. As in the case of "us," Australians, descriptivization is used in relation to positive reactions ("is confident," "is disposed to high migration").

Least often activated, and hence most backgrounded, are the actions of the migrants themselves. They are activated in only 20 percent of cases, mostly in the first twelve lines, that is, in their interactions with "racists" in other countries, where they "tell lies," "press for the right to have Mounties in turbans," "bring bulging wallets," etc. A few of the deactivations descriptivize their actions, represent their actions as more or less permanent characteristics—negative ones: they "are users of welfare," "have high unemployment rates." But most of the deactivations are objectivations of that one crucial action, represented in all of its generality: "immigration."

## 5. Deagentialization

Actions and reactions can be *agentialized*, represented as brought about by human agency, or *deagentialized*, represented as brought about in other ways, impervious to human agency—through natural forces, unconscious processes, and so on. I will distinguish three types of deagentialization: *eventuation*, *existentialization*, and *naturalization*.

In the case of *eventuation*, an action or reaction is represented as an event, as something that just "happens," without the involvement of human agency. The question "by whom?" cannot relevantly be asked in connection to it. One of the ways in which this may be realized is through a material process denoting involuntary action, as in the case of "lose" in this example:

3.45  Parents lose key role in policy making.

Many such processes have an inherently passive sense (e.g., "undergo," "experience," "suffer"), even though, grammatically, they are active:

3.46  They received a sudden cold-shoulder from neighbours and co-workers.

Another possible realization combines objectivation with generalized processes such as "happen" or occur":

> 3.47 Such participation does not seem to happen at senior school.
> 3.48 Signs of fatigue occurred regardless of preschool experience.

Many of the things we might ordinarily think of as events can also be represented as actions, and vice versa. Compare, for instance, the following two examples;

> 3.49 Cohen found that, at the beginning of the trial, the subjects' eyes were fixated at the center of the screen. When a small object was presented at the left or the right of the screen, subjects moved their eyes to read this digit.
> 3.50 When an object begins to move across the field of view, the eyes will begin to move after it after a time interval of about 0.15 seconds.

Example 3.49, an extract from a scientific paper, represents human action ("a small object was presented") and their actor ("Cohen"). Example 3.50, an extract from an introductory textbook, represents an event (the "object moves") and removes the traces of the human experimenter/observer without whose actions, in the end, no representation of natural events is possible.

Conversely, human social practices can serve as a model for representing natural events. Susan Sontag (1979: 64) has pointed out how the representation of cancer is frequently modeled on military practices:

> Cancer cells do not simply multiply, they are "invasive." ... They "colonize" from the original tumor to far sites in the body, first setting up tiny outposts ("metastases").

And, as Freud (1975 [1901]: 221) has shown, what most of us think of as chance accidents can also be represented as brought about by human agency:

> [Bungled actions] prove to be governed by an intention and achieve their aims with a certainty which cannot in general be credited to our conscious voluntary movements.

The English language provides resources for representing processes as either actions or events. But it cannot determine which phenomena should be interpreted as actions and which as events. The same occurrences can readily be represented either as actions or as events, either as voluntary ("the subjects moved their eyes") or as involuntary ("the eye moves"). Both options are, in principle, always open. Contextual, not ontological, factors decide which is taken up in any given instance. This is why I use "transformational" terms in both cases, for agentialization and for eventuation.

In the case of *existentialization*, an action or reaction is represented as something that "simply exists." The action or reaction itself is objectivated and fills the slot of the "existent" (the entity predicated to exist) in "existential clauses," clauses which assert the existence of something and frequently begin with "there" ("there is…," "there exists…"; Halliday, 1985: 130), as in 3.51. Alternatively, existentialization is realized in objectivated ways, e.g., through nominalizations like "existence" 3.52:

3.51  They believed that the immigration program existed for the benefit of politicians, bureaucrats, and the ethnic minorities.
3.52  The very existence of obligatory schools divides any society in two realms.

In the case of *naturalization*, an action or reaction is represented as a natural process by means of abstract material processes, such as "vary," "expend," "develop," etc., which link actions and reactions to specific interpretations of material processes—to discourses of rise and fall, ebb and flood; of birth and death, growth and decay; of change and development and evolution; of fusion and disintegration, expansion and contraction:

3.53  Tolerance is wearing thin.
3.54  All that is changing.

Again, objectivated naturalizations are common. The following example combines existentialization ("a change is coming") with an objectivated naturalization ("changes"):

3.55  With these changes is coming a change in community attitudes.

Naturalization is the most common form of deagentialization in the "Race Odyssey" text, and the writer uses it to give his predictions an air of inevitability: racism is "developing," "debates" are "building," and, the most frequent naturalization, "changes" are "coming."

## 6. Generalization and Abstraction

Different representations may *generalize* actions and reactions to different degrees. What in 3.56 is generalized ("milk time"), for instance, is in 3.57 broken down into several more specific actions ("gathering on the rug," "naming a color," "fetching the milk"):

3.56  Milk time is treated as a specific event in some classes and passes almost unnoticed in others.
3.57  The whole class is gathered on the rug. The teacher names a color and children who are wearing it fetch their milk.

Taking the two examples together, one could construct a taxonomy (table 3.1). But it would be a taxonomy of a peculiar kind. In most taxonomical diagrams, the terms at the lower nodes would have to be read as subordinate: "gathering on the rug," for example, would have to be read as "a kind of milk time." Here, however, "milk time"

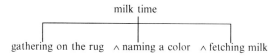

TABLE 3.1. Temporal Composition Taxonomy

generalizes a *sequence* (this is indicated by the carets in the diagram). The diagram can also be seen as a meronymical or "composition" taxonomy in the sense of Martin et al. (1988: 149) except that "composition" is here temporal rather than spatial. "Gathering on the rug," "naming a color," and "fetching the milk" are *parts* of (meronyms of) "milk time." Such temporal composition taxonomies can bring out how the micro-actions which would make up "fetching the milk" (getting up from the rug, walking to the table where the milk is displayed, etc.) constitute "actions," how actions constitute action sequences or "episodes," and how sequences of episodes constitute "practices" (cf. Barthes, 1977: 100ff.). But it is difficult to provide linguistic criteria for recognizing the level of generality of isolated actions such as "gathering on the rug." Generalizations become apparent only in an analysis of the semantic relations between different representations of the same actions and reactions within one text (in which case, it is possible to reconstruct the action taxonomies inherent in that text) or in comparing texts, as I have done informally in this section. Generalization is nevertheless an important issue in critical discourse analysis, as texts which are mainly concerned with legitimizing or delegitimizing actions and reactions tend to move high up on the generalization scale, including only the names of episodes or of whole social practices.

Generalization can be seen as a form of abstraction; they abstract away from the more specific micro-actions that make up actions. Other forms of abstraction abstract *qualities* from actions or reactions. Example 3.58, for instance, abstracts away from the substance of what parents actually do when they "interact" with teachers, suggesting perhaps that it is not important *what* they do, so long as they are seen to "interact with," "relate to," "be involved with" the school. This kind of abstraction I will refer to as *distillation*:

> 3.58 Your interaction with teachers throughout school life can have a very positive effect on your child's attitudes.

Example 3.59, again taken from Illich (1971: 338), abstracts away from what teachers do in order to concentrate on their agentive power:

> 3.59 The teacher exercises a kind of power over their person which is much less limited by constitutional and consuetudinal restrictions than the power wielded by the guardians of other social enclaves.

These distillations not only highlight some aspect of an action at the expense of others, they also realize purposes and legitimations: purposes through the kinds of qualities highlighted (the purposes of soliciting the complicity of parents with the school system and of controlling children, for instance) and legitimations and delegitimations through the evaluative associations which, in the given context, may cling to the terms that establish the reference to the action or reaction. "Involvement," "interaction," and so on have positive connotations in discourses of counseling and therapy, while power may evoke negative connotations, certainly in the context of Illich's *Deschooling Society*, which argues for returning some power to the clients of educational professionals. Since the same qualities can be distilled from a heterogeneous variety of social practices, distillation also allows practices to be compared and classified along the dimensions of quality highlighted by the distillation. Fields of social practice in which the same kinds of purposes and the same kinds of values and disvaluations obtain can thus be demarcated. And such fields are served by the institutions whose (theoretical) practices of distillation elaborate these purposes and values: individual psychologies in the case of "interaction," "involvement," etc.; critical sociologies in the case of "power," "control," etc. Such discourses teach us to see the qualities in a heterogeneous variety of social practices and supply the legitimations and purposes that support these practices—or the delegitimations that allow their critique.

Some of the models of representing actions and reactions that we have already discussed also involve abstraction. The following combination of objectivation and eventuation, for instance, highlights the "ceremonial" quality of the activity of "assembling in the hall":

> 3.60  This ceremony is designed to help the child feel she now belongs to the school.

There is also a metalinguistic form of distillation: the distillation of either the signifier, as in 3.61, or the signified, as in 3.62:

> 3.61  The notion of playtime represents a major discontinuity in the experience of most children starting school.
> 3.62  The term physical education refers to that period of physical activity when the children use specific apparatus and movements to promote muscular coordination and agility.

Distillations in the "Race Odyssey" text include "backlash," "freeze out," "besiege," "disharmony"—all distilling the negative aspect of actions the precise nature of which we can for the most part only guess.

## 7. Overdetermination

In chapter 2, I characterized the symbolic representation of social actors as overdetermination—as a form of representation in which the represented social actors can refer to actual social actors in more than one social practice. Thus, the king of the fairy tale can stand for the father, the company director, or the political leader, and the team of "professional heroes" in westerns (Wright, 1975) for the team of doctors, the team of scientists, the team of presidential aides, and so on. This definition of symbolization can be applied also to social action: the slaying of the dragon in the fairy tale can stand for overcoming the Oedipal conflict, passing the entrance examination, winning the election, in short, for any trial which achieves the goal of a hero's quest. And the killing of the enemy in the western can stand for overcoming, violently or nonviolently, any threat to a society or group, whether disease or disaster, rebellion or crime, or any competition, whether from rival scientists or political opponents. Such stories, set in a fantasy world, a mythical past, or an imagined future, are openly fictional precisely to allow a multiplicity of references, each one as valid as any other. As Wright says of the western: "Myths present *a model of social action* based on mythical interpretation of the past" (1975: 188; emphasis added).

Symbolization can be local or extended, that is, it can extend over all or part of a representation. Allegories, symbolizations extending over the whole of a text, as in fairy tales or westerns, are at the least localized end of the continuum. Metaphorically represented actions, such as "steer" in 3.62 and "build up" in 3.63, are at the local end of the continuum. Note that they differ from the naturalizations and abstractions I discussed earlier: the verbs are concrete material processes which can take only human agents; if used with nonhuman agents, they humanize the natural world, rather than naturalizing the human social world:

3.63  It helps to see yourself as the teacher's partner who can support her efforts to steer your child through the primary skills of learning how to learn.

3.64  She turned the pages with an expert build-up of anticipation.

Like distillations, such metaphors highlight a quality of action rather than representing the action itself. But they do so by means of a concrete image. Also like distillations, they may introduce purposes ('steer' in 3.63, for instance, introduces the purpose of "control") and legitimations (e.g., "build," with its positive connotation, in 3.64), and as a result of their overdetermining potential, they can create covert classifications of action along the dimensions of the quality or qualities highlighted. But, unlike the classifications brought about by distillation, these classifications remain covert. In 3.63, "steering" remains a metaphor, opening up a potential for classification, whereas, say, in Habermas's theory of communicative action (1984), "steering" becomes a major technical term ("steering mechanisms") applicable to social practices in general.

The title of the "Race Odyssey" text is such a symbolization. The archetypal tale of a heroic and perilous journey back home, back to the cradle of one's identity, symbolizes Australians' quest for "racial" identity and connects it to noble quests of this kind generally.

The second form of overdetermination is *inversion*. In "The Story of Asdiwal," Lévi-Strauss (1967) described the role of inversion in a myth of the Tsimshian Indians, a people from the Pacific coast of Canada. The economic activities (fishing, hunting, etc.) represented in this myth accurately describe Tsimshian practices but, says Lévi-Strauss, an anthropologist who would seek to use the myth as evidence for ethnographic description would be bound to make errors, for other Tsimshian practices are inverted in this story. It was, for example, Tsimshian custom for women to move to the village of their husbands after marriage ("patrilocal marriage"), but in "The Story of Asdiwal," the opposite occurs: the hero, Asdiwal, moves to the village of his wife after marriage ("uxorilocal marriage"). Myths, says Lévi-Strauss (1967: 11), "do not give accurate picture[s] of the reality of native life, but a sort of counterpoint which seems sometimes to be in harmony with the reality, and sometimes to part from it." The reason for inversion of this kind lies in the legitimating function of the myth. "The Story of Asdiwal" seeks to legitimize the custom of patrilocal marriage: the hero's deviant actions lead to a crisis which is not resolved until order is restored and the hero lives again in the village of his father: "extreme positions are imagined in order to show that they are untenable" (ibid.: 30).

Comparable inversions occur in "first day" texts. In the children's story I quoted in chapter 2, a little girl takes a lion to school. The lion is not only an inverted participant, he engages in inverted actions, such as "swishing his tail" threateningly during "register time." This creates an incident that disturbs the orderly unfolding of the "register" episode:

> 3.65 The teacher stopped calling the register when she saw the little girl and the lion, and all the other children stared at the lion, wondering what the teacher was going to say. The teacher said to the little girl: "You know you are not allowed to bring pets to school." The lion began to swish his tail—swish!-swash!

When such deviant actions occur, they cause remedial actions or episodes to be inserted into the representation. Unrepentant deviants must be corrected in a punitive episode. Or an attempt must be made "to show that what admittedly appeared to be a threatening expression is really a meaningless event, or an unintentional act, or a joke not meant to be taken seriously, or an unavoidable 'understandable' product of extenuating circumstances" (Goffman, 1974: 223). The teacher training texts in my "first day" corpus provide many instances of this:

> 3.66 The skillful teacher can save the new entrant's face by showing herself to be on his side: "He's not really crying, that's just a noise he's making."

Remedial actions may develop into full-scale social practices and become central in texts dealing with deviant behavior. Newspaper reports on truancy, for instance, often refer to truancy itself only by means of a handful of objectivations ("truancy") and abstractions ("the problem") and concentrate on the social actions which have been institutionalized (or are planned) to counteract it, although there are, of course, also reports which focus on the deviant behavior itself, for instance, by means of short interviews with truant children. The same is true of media representations of many other social problems.

Deviant actions always present a threat to the orderly unfolding of social practices. They reveal the contradictions that underlie these practices, contradictions such as the unequal distribution of the rewards of education among different social groups. On the other hand, representation of deviant action is also attractive, for it allows the vicarious transgression of social norms. Hence, it forms the staple fare of many kinds of texts: news, crime, fiction, gossip, and so on.

The actions of Bruce Roxton, the racist Australians love to hate, are inversions of "correct" social practices. He "damages" and "distorts" and is therefore rightfully "resented" by Australians—but his deviant actions are extensively covered by the Australian media, year after year.

## 8. Conclusion

By way of conclusion, I provide two summaries. Table 3.2 summarizes my answer to the question with which I started and gives an overview of the principal ways

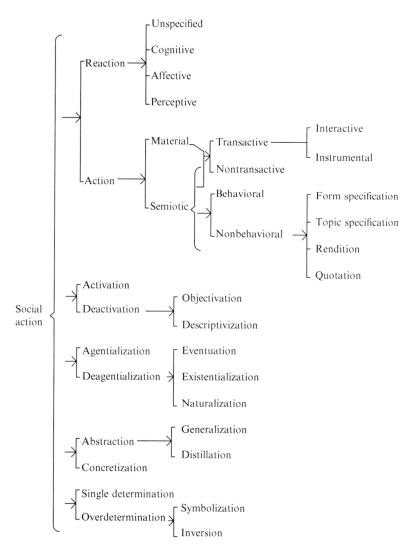

TABLE 3.2.  Social Action Network

in which actions and reactions can be represented in English discourse. As before, square brackets stand for either-or choices (e.g., deactivation can take the form of objectivation or descriptivization), curly brackets for simultaneous choices (e.g., reactions can be activated *and* agentialized, or deactivated *and* agentialized). I will also summarize what this descriptive framework has allowed me to observe about the "Race Odyssey" text.

Both the actions and the reactions of the "racists in other countries" are represented. Their reactions to immigrants and immigration are portrayed as emotive and negative, and their actions are transactive, as actual *interactions* with immigrants— material interactions, such as "attack," as well as behavioralized semiotic interactions, such as "insult." For the most part, these actions and reactions are activated, hence prioritized in the representation.

Australians are also represented as involved in actions and reactions. But Australian reactions are more often portrayed as cognitive, considered, and reasonable, and when they do tend toward the affective and the negative, they are mostly objectivated. The actions of Australians also differ from those of immigration critics in other countries: they tend not to involve interactions with immigrants. Australians are represented as people who stand on the sidelines and monitor the events as they unfold, but not as directly participating in them.

As for the Australian government, both its actions and its reactions are represented, but the former are in the majority. Government action is either semiotic and activated, or material, instrumentalized, and objectivated: what the government says takes center stage; what it does, its instrumentalized transactions with immigrants, remains in the background.

The immigrants themselves are never represented as reacting, and their actions are mostly nontransactive and objectivated. Only the action of "immigrating" itself is represented straightforwardly. Other immigrant actions are veiled behind distillations, such as "freezing out" and "besieging," or behind naturalizations which represent their actions as "change."

Thus, the "Race Odyssey" text allows us to glimpse racist actions in countries other than Australia, but blocks us from access to what happens in Australia itself. Australian "criticism" of immigration takes place at the altogether different level of a reasonable "debate." But it is a debate which keeps a safe distance from what actually goes on in Australia and which refers to actual interactions between Australians and immigrants to Australia only in vague, objectivated, generalized, and abstract ways.

And as far as the immigrants themselves are concerned, their voices are never heard.

# 4

# Time in Discourse

In this chapter, I describe the semiotic resources of English discourse for representing the timing of social practices. My analysis draws on my corpus of "first day at school" texts as well as on an unpublished study of the representation of time in staff newsletters, in-house magazines, and other written internal communications from Rank Xerox (collected in 1995) and in six articles from the *Employment Gazette* (July and September 1993).

## 1. Introduction

In his remarkable book about time, the sociologist Norbert Elias stressed that time, and the way we think and talk about it, is a product of the *activity of timing*—the activity of measuring one kind of activity or event sequence against another kind of activity or event sequence (1992: 43):

> The reifying character of the substantival form "time" disguises the instrumental character of the activity of timing. It obscures the fact that the activity of timing, e.g., by looking at one's watch, has the function of relating to each other the positions of events in the successive order of two or more change continuums.

In this chapter, I focus on the resources which the English language provides for representing this activity. As before, this is not an end in itself, not a labor of classification for its own sake. Sociologists (and also musicologists; see Van Leeuwen, 1999) have drawn attention to the correspondences between the timing of fundamental social activities, on the one hand, and the way people think and talk about time or enact it in symbolic forms, such as music, on the other:

> There is a correspondence, a correlation between a society's economy, the way it organizes work, the means it uses for the production of goods and services, and the way time is represented in the collective consciousness, a representation that every individual receives, internalizes and accepts almost always with no problem. (Grossin, 1990: 307)

A description of the semiotic resources of timing should allow such correspondences to be explored and analyzed in meaningful and enlightening ways and contribute to a better understanding of the fundamental role and power of time in social life.

## 2. The Sociosemantics of Location and Extent

The distinction between "location" and "extent" which underpins Halliday's account of time circumstantials (1985) goes back to the ancient distinction between *kairos*, the "point in time" of an event or activity, and *chronos*, its duration. In my data, I found two fundamental types of timing, both applicable to location and to extent. The first I will refer to as the *time summons*; the second operates on the principle of *synchronization* described by Elias.

### (1) Time Summons

In the *time summons*, timing is represented as being imposed through an authoritative summons. Those on whose activities it is imposed are therefore treated as not being able to, or not being given the means to, anticipate exactly when they are to begin or end a given activity, as having to wait until the word or signal is given, and then obey it.

*Personalized Time Summons*

When a time summons is personalized, it is given by someone who has, in the given context, the right to authoritatively time the activities of another participant or type of participant. This right to time has always been a sign of absolute power. In ancient China, the management of time was a privilege of the emperor, and the same was true in the Roman Empire, to mention just two examples. But, on a smaller scale, the privilege of timing plays a central role in all institutions: the workplace, educational institutions, and, as can be seen in the examples below, the family.

In English, the personalized time summons is typically realized either by a verbal process clause with an authoritative sayer and the timing of the activity as the projected clause, or by an authoritative verbal process in a hypotactic time clause, as in the examples below:

4.1 "It's time to go home," she [a mother] said.

4.2  Management establishes who works when.

4.3  Come when I call.

But authoritative timing may also be realized nonverbally, for instance, through gestures, in some cases, e.g., conducting an orchestra, in very fine detail.

In the "first day at school" data, children's activities are frequently represented as timed in this way, with mothers and teachers (or more experienced school friends) as the authority. Contemporary "flexible work patterns" also reintroduce the time summons, with managers, "team leaders," etc., disrupting internalized time disciplines and rhythms of work, for instance, with authoritative deadlines. Negt (1984: 84) has described this process and its negative effect on workers who are now "subject to the changes and transformations dictated by the contingencies of the moment," which they themselves can neither observe nor anticipate.

### Instrumentalized Time Summons

As already indicated, a time summons may also be "instrumentalized," as in the case of the alarm clock, the school bell, the church bell, the factory whistle, the traffic light, and so on. Here, the power of timing becomes impersonal and institutionalized and hence, to some extent, naturalized.

Linguistic representations of the instrumentalized time summons will, typically, be realized through a material process clause with the signaling instrument as actor and the signaling as process (or a passive version: "the signal was given"):

4.4  The final bell rang, and it was time to go home.

### Disembodied Time Summons

A final kind of time summons has a more intangible source of authority, time itself. This can be variously interpreted as a kind of internalized sense of timing ("I will know when the time comes"), as a kind of inescapable fate, or as a form of timing ordained by time itself. Silke Kirschner (2003) has analyzed how George W. Bush used the disembodied time summons in the run-up to the Iraq war, in which timing was a crucial aspect of the process and an equally crucial signifier of American power.

In English, the disembodied time summons is typically realized by an "existential" time clause, or a clause in which time itself is agentive, as in the following examples:

4.5  It was time to dress.

4.6  The great day came.

### (2)  Synchronization

*Synchronization* is timing by reference to "the successive order of events in some other change continuum," as Elias put it (1992: 43). In other words, here the location and/or extent of social activities are timed in relation to other social activities, or to events in the natural world, or to artificially created events, such as the passing of time on a clock. Each of these allows for measurement and for time spans of different levels of magnitude, e.g., according to the way social activities punctuate time (from the rhythms of daily activities to the "stages of life") or the rhythms of nature (days, moons, seasons, etc.).

### Social Synchronization

In social synchronization, activities are synchronized with other social activities. They start and end at the same time (or before, or after) other social activities. In contrast to clock time, this involves awareness of the social environment, attentiveness to what other people are doing. In strictly clock-oriented environments, it stands little chance: students begin to pack up their papers when the hour approaches, not when the lecturer's discourse begins to display signs of drawing to a close. But in environments where team work or social companionship are important, it can move to the foreground, as in music radio programming with its "breakfast" and "drive time" programs. In my "first day" data, it occurs mainly in relation to young children, who are thereby treated as not yet having much sense of clock time, or as living, as yet, only in the moment.

Typically, the activity with which the timed activity is to be synchronized is realized as a hypotactic time clause, or as a circumstantial with time as head and the activity as classifier, or as token, with the timed activity as value as, e.g., in the following examples:

> 4.7  It [the teacher reading a story to the class] is a good moment for mothers to hug their child and slip away.
> 4.8  By lunchtime they were ready to go.
> 4.9  You have to wait until we get back.

### Natural Synchronization

Here, activities are synchronized with natural events, starting or ending (or lasting as long as) specific observable phenomena in the natural environment (the movement of planets and stars, the flight of birds, etc.) as, e.g., in recipes (although the timing of recipes can also be formulated in terms of mechanized time):

> 4.10  When the mixture is bubbling, tip in all the flour.

Natural synchronization has been, and still is, of fundamental importance in many cultures, often mediated by priests, astrologers, and so on. In contemporary Western culture, it has often become marginalized (e.g., astrology) or highly specialized (e.g., scientific observation), and may even conflict with the demands of the workplace:

> 4.11  Whoever wants to go on vacation when the weather is nice is persuaded not to do it because right at that time important orders could come in.

However, natural synchronization has not disappeared from people's consciousness and plays an important role in discourses that look back to an age when time was a "sequence of experiences" and that lament the way in which the clock has "dissociated time from organic sequences," so that "one does not go to bed with the chickens on a winter's night, but invents wicks, chimneys, lamps, gaslights, electric lights, so as to use all the hours of the day" (Mumford, 1934: 17).

In my data, which mostly relate to the timing practices of dominant institutions such as work and school, there are only a handful of instances of natural synchronization, and it is therefore not possible to generalize here about the linguistic realization of this sociosemantic category.

## Mechanical Synchronization

Mechanical synchronization results from practices of calculating time and devising instruments that provide artificial events with which human actions can be synchronized. It is this kind of timing which, predictably, attracts most comment in the literature. Historians, philosophers, sociologists, and anthropologists have all expressed deep unease with the way mechanized time has come to dominate social practices over the past 200 years or so, and they often express nostalgia for times and places where the tyranny of the clock did not exist:

> Abstract time became the new medium of existence. Organic functions themselves were regulated by it: one ate, not upon feeling hungry, but when prompted by the clock; one slept, not when one was tired, but when the clock sanctioned it. (Mumford, 1934: 17)

> The Nuer have no expression equivalent to "time" in our language, and they cannot, therefore, speak of time as though it were something which passes, can be wasted, saved, and so forth.... Events follow a logical order, but they are not controlled by an abstract system, there being no autonomous point of reference to which activities have to conform with precision. (Evans-Pritchard, 1940: 103)

Predictably, mechanical synchronization is the most frequent category in my data, usually realized by circumstantials with "at," "on," and "by," or by pre- or postmodification, as in the following examples:

4.12  They arrived at school at 9:30 a.m.
4.13  Children were admitted on 5 September.
4.14  They had a two-week break.

## (3) Punctuality

The ascendance of mechanized time in the industrial era came with an increased emphasis on *punctuality*—and an increased anxiety about starting activities or getting to places exactly on time. But even in the most punctual societies, different social practices are associated with different punctuality rules. Leisure activities, for instance, require less punctuality than work activities, and it may even be embarrassing to arrive too punctually at an evening social occasion. The same relative freedom from punctuality was also realized in the music of the industrial age. While public, "heroic" music was increasingly subject to "metronomic" time and to the strict synchronization of all players or singers to the same beat, in *Lieder*, or romantic piano music, composed for salon performance, "suspension, delaying the beat, became one of the key affective devices—*stretching* time, so as to escape its rigidities, if only for a moment, and only within the context of leisure time and the private sphere" (Van Leeuwen, 1999: 58).

In my data, punctuality expresses itself for the most part in relational clauses with a punctuality attribute ("late," "early," "on time," "on schedule," etc.) or in circumstantials, as in the following examples:

4.15  We are going to be late for dinner.

4.16  We should be arriving well on schedule.

4.17  I'm sure it's not too early to wish you a merry Christmas.

4.18  Far too early, they started out.

4.19  Working mothers cannot be home in time to meet their youngsters.

(4)  Exact and Inexact Timing

Timing may be exact (e.g., "at six o'clock") or inexact. The latter includes cases where timing is still regulated but in a relatively relaxed way (e.g., "during the night," "from time to time") and cases of deregulated, "flexible" timing, where timing is represented as not regulated at all.

Regulated inexact timing is expressed by indefiniteness, by a relatively circumscribed vocabulary of indefinite time words and expressions or by diluting exact time expressions with modifiers (e.g., "some time during the afternoon," "by approximately the middle of the afternoon"). Inexact extent is realized by duration epithets such as "long," "short," etc. ("a quick look at the paper," "a long journey"), and indefinite time circumstantials ("for a while," "for some time," etc.). Even though my data do not contain enough examples to generalize about the realization of deregulated inexact timing, it seems nevertheless an important category, especially in discourses where institutions, whether schools or companies, seek to portray a friendly and flexible image, and in discourses addressed to consumers, where "choice" has become a linchpin ideological category. Here are a few examples:

4.20  Drinking time is flexible: any time during the morning.

4.21  Save and Prosper Direct is open when it suits you.

4.22  People learn when and where suits them best.

4.23  Study at the time, place, and pace which satisfies your circumstances and requirements.

(5)  Unique and Recurring Timing

Finally, timing can be *unique*, pertaining only to a single instance of an activity, or *recurring*, pertaining to every instance (or most instances) of a given activity. In my data, texts addressing children often represent timings as unique, with the effect,

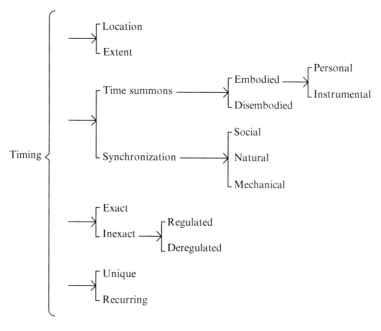

TABLE 4.1. Timing Network

perhaps, that children are represented as unable to understand recurrence (the point is often made that they do not at first realize that they will have to go to school every day). Texts addressing teachers, on the other hand, represent timings as recurrent, as "schedules." Again, power and status determine the degree to which discourses provide access to the means of generalizing experience.

Typical realizations include premodifiers and adjuncts ("daily," "weekly," etc.) and time expressions preceded by universal pronouns, such as "each" and "every." In an environment of habituality, all time expressions become recurring:

    4.24  It was practice for children in infant schools to be given free milk daily.
    4.25  Annual transfer was easier to cope with.
    4.26  Assembly usually occurs at the start of the day.

We can now summarize the discussion in this section in a system network (table 4.1).

## 3. Experiencing Duration

In the course of the nineteenth century, as the grip of the clock on society tightened, people increasingly began to contrast the subjective *experience* of time with the "objective" reality of clock time. Philosophers wrote about it (e.g., Bergson, 1966), psychological novels capitalized on it, and in films, with their ability to stretch or condense time through editing, subjective time played a key role in storytelling. Spans of time, people realized, which according to the clock last for a long time, can be experienced as flashing by in an instant, and vice versa. In my data, this contrast crops up regularly, especially in "first day" texts for children, which often mention that the first day "was over before they knew it" (and hence experienced as positive and exciting). For critical discourse analysis, it is important to investigate to which of the participants in a social practice feelings and subjective experiences are ascribed, and to which they are not. Generally, this relates to power. The regulators of social practices want people not only to *do* the right thing, but also to identify with it, to "own it," in the contemporary jargon. Regulating discourses therefore emphasize the feelings and subjective experiences of citizens, customers, patients, students, etc., while the feelings of government officials, managers, doctors, or teachers receive less attention and are treated as irrelevant, with the notable exception of their ubiquitous "concern" for the interests of their citizens, customers, and so on.

Linguistically, the subjective experience of time is realized in terms of the duration of activities (typically through time circumstantials, and through relational clauses in which the activity is the carrier and the speed of time the attribute), or in terms of experiencing the duration of time itself (typically through clauses in which time itself is the actor and the speed of time a circumstantial):

4.27  Before they knew it, they were following her down a long corridor.
4.28  Though it [the first day at school] seemed long, it wasn't really.
4.29  The days dragged by so slowly.
4.30  The morning passed very quickly.

## 4. Managing Time

So far, I have focused on the timing of social practices, but timing itself is also a social practice—an *integrative* practice, vital for the coherence of social life, for holding together most, if not all, of the social practices of a society. Elias (1992) and others have described the history of what we would now call *time management* as a history in which time has been parceled up in ever-smaller units of time, and in which the balance has gradually moved from natural synchronization to arbitrary decisions (and hence to human power) and to technologies of mechanical synchronization. The day, for instance, is a unit of time still grounded in natural synchronization, but the week of seven days is not; it is a cultural construct, taken over from the Jews and authoritatively imposed by Julius Caesar. When the Romans introduced the sundial in the third century B.C., people already complained about the arbitrary tyranny of time, but many centuries had still to pass before the introduction of the minute regimes of scheduling described by Foucault in *Discipline and Punish* (1979: 150–51):

> Activities were governed in detail by orders that had to be obeyed immediately....In the early nineteenth century, the following time-table was suggested for the *Ecoles Mutuelles*, or "mutual improvement schools": 8.45 entrance of the monitor, 8.52 the

monitor's summons, 8.56 entrance of the children and prayer, 9.00 the children go to their benches, 9.04 first slate, 9.08 end of dictation, 9.12 second slate, etc. . . . But attempts were also made to assure the quality of the time used: constant supervision, the pressure of supervisors, the elimination of anything that might disturb or distract. . . . Time measured and paid for must also be a time without impurities or defects.

## Scheduling Time

The business of scheduling time is the business of fixing and regulating, by whatever method, when things are done and for how long. Contrary to, for instance, the Hopi language, as described by Whorf (1956), contemporary English has many ways of representing acts of scheduling, usually by means of "scheduling processes," such as "schedule," "fix," "regulate," "appoint," etc., with the scheduler as actor, some time expression (time itself, or a given period of time) as goal, and the activity itself included as a circumstance of purpose or a beneficiary:

> 4.31 Time can be allocated or reallocated to different leisure activities, in what we label the "intro-activity" allocation process.
> 4.32 The individual will seek to expand the time available for more desirable activities.

The all-powerful agent of the process may, of course, also be deleted by means of passive agent deletion:

> 4.33 Business hours have been increased.

## Budgeting Time

Many commentators have noted how time can be discursively equated with spending money, and represented as a form of close accounting. This involves "time budget processes," such as "save," "spend," "squander," "fritter away," etc., with time, or some unit of mechanical time, as goal:

> 4.34 I seem to be running out of time constantly.
> 4.35 The possession of time-saving devices such as a washing machine or a microwave oven indicates a desire to use wealth to save time.

## Transforming Time

At present, time management is in transition in many spheres of society. Temporal location is fragmented, with specific activities occurring at many different times, and other units (units of work, credit points, etc.) being superimposed on, or supplanting, time units as measures of extent. It is therefore now possible to speak of the "staggering" or "spreading" of activities and of the "fragmenting," "pluralizing," and "destructuralizing" of time, to give just some examples.

Social commentators have compared this new regime of time to the way women handle time in domestic work (Nowotny, 1984) and to preindustrial ways of handling time. Now, as then, they say, there is "less separation between work and life; social relationships and work are intertwined, and the work day lengthens and shortens according to the tasks to be performed" (Thompson, 1967: 70). Others have argued that this is, in effect, a return to authoritative timing (e.g., Negt, 1984). But history does not repeat itself. We are not returning to preindustrial timing, but moving toward postindustrial timing. While large, dominating clocks are disappearing from the streets and the walls and mantelpieces of our homes, the clock is still there, now less obtrusively, integrated into a wide range of objects linked to different activities: video recorders, cars, computers, and so on. The personal watch remains as vital as ever. Time in the postindustrial age is fragmented and multiple, but I can see no evidence that new principles of timing are emerging. It is the uses and relative importance of the principles that are changing. The synchronization of everyone to the same beat (everyone working the same hours, listening to the news at the same time, taking holidays at the same time, and so on) is gradually disappearing. Society has become polyrhythmic. In the vacuum created by the disappearance of universal and taken-for-granted rules of clock time, authoritative timing may reassert itself in places where it is no longer needed. But this creates friction and conflict. The solution has to lie elsewhere. Temporal coherence in a polyrhythmic society will have to rely more on social timing. In his excellent book on polyrhythmic music, Chernoff (1979) describes how, in polyrhythmic music, coherent music making does not depend on simultaneous starts and endings, nor on all musicians sticking to the same beat. Instead, all players use their own timing. In this sense, polyrhythmic music celebrates individuality and difference, "pluralism as a source of vitality," as Chernoff says (1979: 158)—and he adds that this kind of pluralism is a key value in many African societies, which see the world as a place where multiple forces act together in determining what should and does happen, and when. But paradoxically, this also involves heightened awareness of the other musicians, of the social group, one could say. Without the whole, says Chernoff, the individual parts would "give the impression of a rhythm tripping along clumsily or meaninglessly accented" (1979: 52). In polyrhythmic music, the "beat," the temporal principle of musical and social cohesion, emerges from the way the different individual rhythms engage and communicate with each other.

Music often heralds changes in society. Perhaps the increasing importance of rhythm in popular music and the increasing popularity of polyrhythmic music herald changed modes of social timing that will rely much more on social interaction, and much less on authoritarian principles, or on the mechanical principle of the clock. No doubt, technologies such as mobile phones, which today allow people to be constantly in interaction with each other, will play a key role in this development.

## 5. Two Examples

I will end by applying my categories to some texts from my "first day at school" corpus, beginning with two quite different children's books. *Mark and Mandy*

(Leete-Hodge, n.d.) was bought at a supermarket checkout, shortly before the beginning of the school year. It is a cheaply produced hardcover, with rather lurid color illustrations on every page, and it tells the story of two children who live in city apartments in the same building and who are experiencing the first day at school together. *Mary Kate and the School Bus* (Morgan, 1985) was bought in the children's section of a large bookstore. It is a much more sparsely illustrated paperback, with black-and-white pen drawings every few pages, and it recounts the first school day of a single child who lives with her parents in a large, free-standing house in an English village. Clearly, Mark and Mandy and Mary Kate belong to different social classes, and the ways the two books are produced and marketed suggest that they are aimed at parents of different social classes also. The schools also differ. Mark and Mandy's school is surprisingly old-fashioned and disciplinarian, while Mary Kate's school has more room for individual play and individual attention to each child. The following extract from *Mark and Mandy* contains quite a few time expressions. There are authoritative time summonses (the teacher's announcement that "school is just about to begin," the bell ringing). There is some stress on the importance of punctuality, of being "on time." And the children's subjective experience of time is emphasized ("before they knew it"):

4.36  A smiling teacher met them at the door.
"Come along, Mandy and Mark," she said. "I'll show you where to put your coats."
And before they knew it, they were following her down a long corridor to a cloakroom full of chattering voices.
"Here you are," she said. "Number 23 and 24."
They hung up their coats and looked at each other.
"Hurry up now, everyone," said the teacher. "School is just about to begin."
Suddenly a bell began to ring and children came running from all directions so as to be in their places on time.

The equivalent episode from *Mary Kate and the School Bus* is too long to reproduce here in full, but a section will give an impression—and show that timing is much less central here. Time is represented as a sequence of events, without indications of location and extent:

4.37  Miss Laurie showed Mary Kate a little table and chair. "You can sit here," she said.
"There's a drawer to put your things in and this is so you won't forget where you are." She took a card out of a box and fixed it firmly to a corner of the table with four big drawing pins. It was a picture of a red elephant, just like the one in the cloakroom.
"Now I'll just get a card for your name," said Miss Laurie, looking in another box.
"Then I'll go and ring the bell and let the others in. Now, what shall I put on this card? What do they call you at home?"
"Mary Kate," said Mary Kate, surprised, wondering what else they could call her.
"Right," said Miss Laurie, "that's what we'll call you then. That way we shan't muddle you up with the other Mary."

Mary Kate said nothing. She wasn't sure she liked the idea of another Mary.

Miss Laurie went out of the room and a moment later Mary Kate heard the clanging of a bell close by. The noise was so loud she had to put her hands over her ears to shut it out.

Then the children came in, talking and laughing and pushing at one another. They clattered into the classroom and made their way to their places, all staring at Mary Kate as they passed her.

The most frequent time expressions in the *Mark and Mandy* book as a whole are expressions of the subjective experience of time (50 percent) and time summonses (27 percent). The punctuality expression in the extract above is the only example in the book. In *Mary Kate*, social synchronization dominates (78 percent), and there is more emphasis on punctuality: Mary Kate constantly misjudges timings, thinking, for instance, that it is time to go home when it is not. To sum up, the lower of the two class positions correlates with externally imposed timing and with subjective alienation from that timing. The higher-class position correlates with a lack of externally imposed timing and the as-yet-unsuccessful internalization of time, showing that school timing is recontextualized differently in the two instances, representing the different habituses of different class positions.

As a second example, I compare these two books together with a long chapter from a text which is written for teachers and which outlines procedures for dealing with children (and parents) on the first day at school on the basis of a survey of current practices (Cleave et al., 1982). The short extract below gives an indication of the style—and the text's insistence on intricate timing details, many of them relying on mechanical synchronization:

4.38  Assembly is a gathering together of all or part of the school to worship God. For practical reasons it is usually held in the school hall. It occurs at the start of the day or at some time during the morning, more rarely in the afternoon. The nursery class may be included once a week or less. It lasts from about ten to thirty minutes. Parents are sometimes invited, either regularly or on special occasions.

Looking at the two (sets of) texts as a whole, rather than at the extracts only, shows that in the teacher training text more activities are timed (64 percent versus 24 percent), with mechanical synchronization accounting for over half the timings (though in a much more flexible way than in the early nineteenth-century *écoles mutuelles*), while in the children's books mechanical synchronization is virtually absent. The children's books contain many time summonses, the teacher training text only two. The children's books do not use recurrent timing, while in the teacher text it is dominant. While there are no instances of experienced duration in the teacher training text, in the children's books they are very frequent. Finally, there are, predictably, no instances of "managing time" in the children's books (though there is, as we have seen, some emphasis on punctuality in *Mary Kate*), while in the teacher text, time management expressions are frequent, but punctuality taken for granted.

Although all of these texts deal with the same practice, and although they all stem from the same country and period, they recontextualize the practice differently, this time not on the basis of social class, but on the basis of power. Teachers are represented as in control of timing; indeed, it is the purpose of the text to instruct them in the exercise of that control. Their feelings, their subjective experiences of time, are considered to be irrelevant. Children, on the other hand, are at the receiving end of the teacher's control over time. What in the teacher text is *not* represented as based on authority becomes, from the child's point of view, authoritarian, a "time summons," and children are represented as lacking the means to understand timing—lacking an understanding of mechanical synchronization, lacking the means to generalize the timing of events as recurrent, and so on. As a result, they can only experience timing subjectively or, as in Mary Kate's case, fail to anticipate it correctly. It is hoped that these brief examples demonstrate what can be done with the kind of sociosemantic tools I have presented here.

# 5

# Space in Discourse

In this chapter, I describe how the spaces in which social practices are acted out can be, and are, represented in English discourse and also in visual images. Both my linguistic and visual examples draw on the "first day at school" corpus.

## 1. Introduction

Most approaches to space and language continue to be inspired by the philosophy of Immanuel Kant, who saw space as one of the basic a priori—and universal—principles of human cognition. Here, I explore a different point of view, the point of view that our understandings of space derive from and can be linked directly to social action, to the way in which we use space in acting out social practices. A look at the history of maps can illustrate this point. Figure 5.1 shows how early maps explicitly represented space as a setting for complex actions and included spatial information only insofar as it was relevant to these actions.

In the early days of modern science, maps played a key role in practices of seafaring, trade, and colonialism and still included pictorial elements, for instance, pictures of ships. But gradually, action was left out and space came to be represented as an objective order, existing separately from, and prior to, human action. Kay O'Halloran (2005) has described how the same process took place in the development of mathematical drawings. For the sixteenth-century scientist Tartaglia, geometry, the science of space, was fully engaged with the social actions it sought to understand and improve (figure 5.2). Geometry was depicted in its social context. Less than a century later, it would abstract away from the social actions which, of course, it continued to serve (figure 5.3).

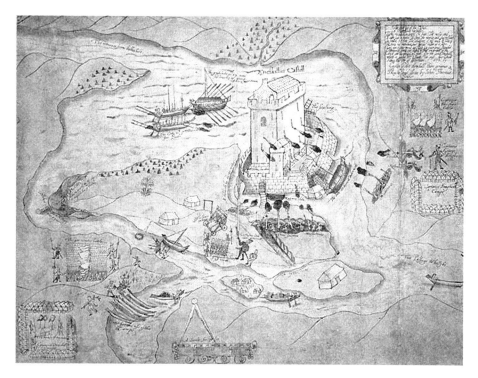

FIGURE 5.1. Early map. Cotton Augustus I.ii, 39. Permission granted by British Library.

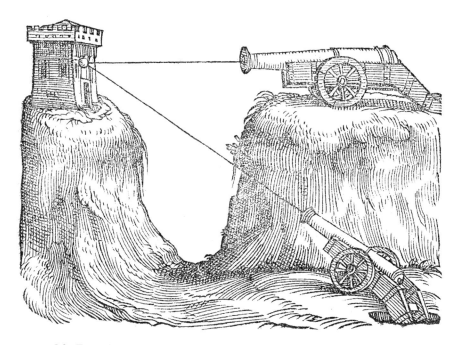

FIGURE 5.2. Tartaglia's drawing of hitting a target (1546). Reproduced by courtesy of the University Librarian and Director, John Rylands University Library, University of Manchester.

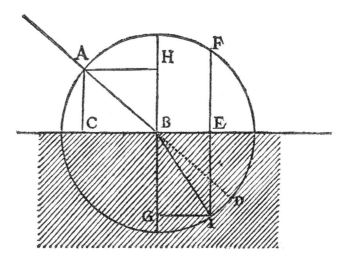

FIGURE 5.3. Circles and lines (Descartes, 1628). Reproduced by
courtesy of the University Librarian and Director, John Rylands
University Library, University of Manchester.

Foucault's influential book *Discipline and Punish* (1979) explored the use of
space for enforcing and maintaining power relations. "Whenever one is dealing with
a multiplicity of individuals on whom a task or a particular form of behavior must
be imposed," he wrote in his discussion of Bentham's Panopticon, "the panoptic
schema may be used....It is the diagram of a mechanism of power reduced to its
ideal form" (1979: 205). Today, the principle of the Panopticon continues to be an
important management tool. Eley and Marmot (1995: 76), in a book subtitled "What
Every Manager Needs to Know about Offices," write that good teamwork is "encouraged in locations where lines of sight and access routes on the office floor link many
workplaces," and the German management consultant Boje (1971: 64) writes that
open offices create "a new type of office user," who "speaks more softly, is more con-
siderate, dresses correctly and carefully and conducts arguments at a calmer pitch."
Clearly, a critical analysis of power should not ignore the fundamental role of space
in enacting social practices: "The material environment predisposes us in very specific, important and lasting ways in our doings and sayings" (Iedema, 2000: 65).
Here, however, my focus is on the construction of space in *discourse*. I am assuming
that discourses about space provide normative understandings of space and of its use
in controlling social practices. To be able to study this, we need to understand the
"grammar of space," the resources we have for representing space in discourse.

## 2. Locating Action

*Space*, in this chapter, includes both the natural or constructed layout of spatial settings and the fixtures in those settings, such as trees, or furniture, or pictures on the

walls. But it does not include "props," objects that are used to perform some part of the social practice. The "charts and pictures" in 5.1, for instance, are part of the setting, but the "audiovisual aids" in 5.2 are not, as they are used as *resources* (see chapter 1) for enacting the social practice.

5.1 Charts and pictures adorn the walls.
5.2 Audiovisual aids such as televisions and tape recorders are frequently used.

Many representations of space and spatial arrangements are directly linked to actions. This involves both the *positions* taken during a particular stage of the social practice and the *transitions* between such stages.

Positions provide an explicit representation of the spatial arrangement for a social practice or a stage thereof. This may range from body positions, such as standing or sitting, to indications of a location, such as "in school" or "at home." Transitions, similarly, provide an explicit representation of the transition from the space of one social practice or part thereof to that of the next. They may be as minimal as a change of posture, e.g., standing up or sitting down, or involve a larger or smaller change of location.

Positions are linguistically realized either by circumstances of location (rest), that is, by locative phrases with prepositions indicating a static location, such as "in" and "at," or by what we could call "position processes," such as "sitting on," "flanked by," etc.:

5.3 Each activity is carried out at a special table.
5.4 The teacher is backed by a shining collage of gold and silver foil and flanked by bookshelves.
5.5 Assembly is usually held in the school hall.

Visually, positions are realized by what, in film language, is called an "establishing shot," a picture that shows the whole of a location, insofar as it is relevant to the action, and thereby allows subsequent detail shots to be "placed" in the whole by the viewer. The concept can also be applied to still pictures, as in figure 5.4.

Transitions are linguistically realized by circumstances of location (motion), that is, by phrases with prepositions that realize motion to or from a location, such as "toward," "to," "from," or by what we might call "motion + location" processes, such as "enter," "gather around," etc.:

5.6 They entered the classroom.
5.7 The children gather around their teacher.
5.8 The teacher removed him to a place beside her desk.

Visually, transitions are realized by movement from one position to another. In film, this is typically accompanied by the camera panning or tracking along with the movement, but still pictures can depict movement too (figure 5.5).

Both "positions" and "transitions" (and also the "descriptions" I will discuss in section 4) can be further located by being given a *setting*. The setting relates a located action to an adjoining location, or to the whole of which it forms a part. Linguistically, this is realized by double circumstances of location (e.g., "on a chair"

**Tell the story**

FIGURE 5.4.  Visual position (Ladybird, 1977: 49). Illustration
from *Talkabout Starting School* by Margaret West and Ethel
Wingfield © Ladybird Books, Ltd., 1977. Reproduced by kind
permission of Ladybird Books, Ltd.

and "in the middle of the room" in example 5.9) or by spatial anchoring processes
such as "adjoin," "be nearby," etc.:

5.9    Mrs. Thompson seats herself on a chair in the middle of the room.
5.10  She was fast asleep on the floor by the doll's house.
5.11  The toilets are a long way from the classroom, in a separate block.

FIGURE 5.5. Visual transition (Ladybird, 1977: 4). Illustration from *Talkabout Starting School* by Margaret West and Ethel Wingfield © Ladybird Books, Ltd., 1977. Reproduced by kind permission of Ladybird Books, Ltd.

Visually, settings are realized by the presence of foreground and background. Figure 5.4 is an example, as it shows both the spatial arrangement with the teacher on a chair and the children on the floor, and the classroom setting. Figure 5.6 only shows the spatial arrangement and leaves out the setting.

So far, the discursive construction of social space may seem a straightforward matter of indicating where and in what kind of spatial arrangements things happen. But it is not necessarily as simple as that.

The floor plan in figure 5.7 is taken from a study of the transition from home to school (Cleave et al., 1982) which combines ethnographic description with precepts and best practice examples for teachers. It shows an actual class and is recommended, in the accompanying text, because it contains elements with which children will be familiar from nursery school, which, it is said, will help them to settle in more easily.

I drew the floor plan in figure 5.8 on the basis of the following passage from a children's book (Morgan, 1985: 28):

FIGURE 5.6.  Position without setting (Ladybird, 1977, front cover).
Illustration from *Talkabout Starting School* by Margaret West and
Ethel Wingfield © Ladybird Books, Ltd., 1977. Reproduced by
kind permission of Ladybird Books, Ltd.

5.12  The classroom had big windows, set high in the wall. Through one of them Mary Kate
could see the top of a tree and a patch of sky and through the other she could see the
church tower. All round the walls were paintings and drawings and big coloured diagrams
and pictures. In one corner was a doll's house and a cot with a doll in it and in another
was a table piled with books. There was a stove with a huge fireguard round it and, most
wonderful of all, there was a little playhouse, with windows and a door and real curtains.

Although I tried to draw only what was in the text, this was not entirely possible.
The text does not indicate the shape of the classroom, for instance, yet I needed to draw

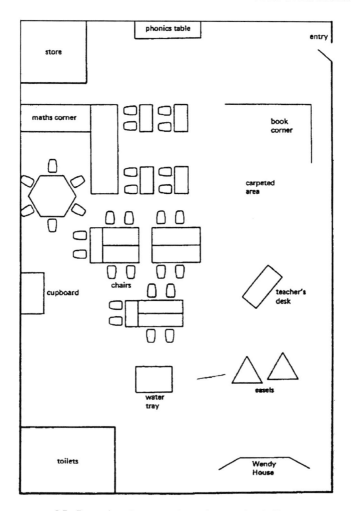

FIGURE 5.7.  Reception class room in a primary school (Cleave et al., 1982: 53).

corners to place the doll's house in a corner. I also wanted to bring out the similarities between the two floor plans. But the drawing will illustrate my point: the description in the story is selective. It includes what the child already knows from home or nursery school (maybe with the exception of the "table piled with books") and leaves out the new and unfamiliar, especially the fact that the room is arranged for a whole *class* of children. Yet figure 5.7 also leaves things out—the "paintings and…big coloured diagrams and pictures," for instance. It shows only the horizontal dimension of space, the dimension of action and functionality, and not the vertical dimension, the symbolic dimension. In the linguistic description, these two are intertwined.

In short, the discursive construction of social space is not necessarily informed only by a concern to indicate where things are located, not just a matter of adding some "reality indices" (Barthes, 1977) to provide a sense of setting and atmosphere.

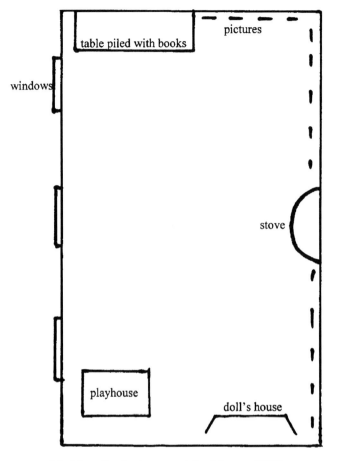

FIGURE 5.8. Mary Kate's classroom (after Morgan, 1985).

It is informed also by the functions and meanings of space. When we read that "each activity is carried out at a special table," we do not learn much about location. What we do learn is that different activities are to be kept quite separate and that activities take place at tables, not on the floor, that a certain discipline is imposed on playing which does not exist at home, and that this discipline is largely imposed by the spatial arrangement of the classroom.

Again, when we learn that the teacher is "backed by a shining collage of gold and silver foil" and "flanked by bookshelves," the point is not so much to tell us exactly where the teacher is, but to emphasize her authority, to endow her with the symbolic attributes of royalty (gold and silver) and learning (books).

## 3. Arranging and Interpreting Space

In an account of English classrooms in inner-city London high schools, Kress et al. (2005) describe how teachers use space to establish particular relations with their students and to control what should and what should not happen in class. Different teachers, they show, do this in different ways. Some classrooms used a traditional "transmission" approach, with individual student tables lined up in rows. In another class, which they describe as "participatory/authoritarian," tables were put together to create teams of four to five students facing each other, realizing a participatory "teamwork" approach that differs from the traditional "transmission" approach. But the "participatory" was mixed with the "authoritarian": the students' tables were angled to allow the teacher total visual control from the front of the classroom. This placed strong constraints on the students' posture, at least if they wanted to see the teacher and follow the lesson, so much so that the traditional "transmission" approach would in fact have allowed more postural freedom. The researchers also describe spatial arrangements at the level of body positioning. In one "mixed ability" class, student tables were again put together to form teams of four or five students, but this time according to ability. When the teacher approached a table with "high ability" students, she did not sit down but casually leaned on the table, coming quite close to the students. When she approached a table with "low ability" students, she sat down, which created more distance.

Clearly, if space is functionalized and hierarchized for the purposes of an institutional order, spatial arrangements such as the positioning of tables becomes a particularly important and powerful "preparatory practice" (see chapter 1). In discourse, such activities of *arranging space* are realized by material processes of architecture, interior decoration, furniture arrangement, body positioning, etc. ("hang," "put," "organize," "set up," "situate," "position," "seat," etc.) or, visually, by showing such actions:

> 5.13  Organize space within the base so that children have corners for privacy and quiet.
> 5.14  A friendly and very efficient teacher had set up activities for every child.
> 5.15  Someone had put flowers on the teacher's desk.

*Interpreting space*—normatively and authoritatively assigning functions and meanings to spaces and spatial arrangements—is another important form of social control. *Assigning meanings* is realized by "signification" processes, such as "convey," "signal," etc., or by verbal processes which project signification processes. *Assigning functions* is realized by purpose constructions (see chapter 6) or by visual processes of "showing" and "demonstrating":

> 5.16  She [the teacher] shows her a peg on which to hang her coat.
> 5.17  "There is a drawer to put your things in," she [the teacher] said.
> 5.18  The environment may be intended by adults to convey a specific message.
> 5.19  The mysteries of the dark alcove in the corner and that something called "The Hall" were revealed [by the teacher].

Not all space interpretations nominate who (in the above examples, mostly the teacher) assigns meanings and functions to spaces and spatial arrangements. At times, the meanings and functions are represented as inherent in the spatial environment, so that the environment itself facilitates or controls actions or signifies symbolic meanings.

Such deagentialized space interpretations are realized by processes which have space itself as the actor. They are examples of the category of "spatialization," which I introduced in chapter 3, the case in which a space is substituted for a social actor:

> 5.20  An uninterrupted expanse of floor gave Ian ample opportunity for riding round and round in his favourite pedal car.
> 5.21  The environment signals friendliness and welcome.

This quote from Iedema (2000: 65), which I used in the beginning of this chapter, is another example:

> 5.22  The material environment predisposes us in very specific, important and lasting ways in our doings and sayings.

## 4. Description and Legitimation

Like the examples discussed in section 2, descriptive clauses can also link spatial arrangements and locations to actions, for instance, by coding a space or a spatial fixture or arrangement as carrier or token in a relational clause or as existent in an existential clause, or by coding spatial functions or meanings as attributes or values in relational clauses. In example 5.23, an action is realized as a premodifier in a nominal group, and in 5.24 by substituting a tool for the action in which it is used. Visual descriptions may be realized by pictures focusing on specific parts of spatial settings, or by what Kress and Van Leeuwen (2007) call "symbolic processes," pictures in which an object symbolizes an attribute of a depicted person and in which that object is represented in a visually conspicuous way, for instance, by placing it in the foreground, or by being held in a way that is clearly not related to the normal function of the object. Figure 5.9 is such a descriptive visual.

> 5.23  These are the reception classes, one on each side of the corridor.
> 5.24  Carpeted areas are for floor toys.

Other descriptions do not link to actions in this way and seem to provide description for its own sake, perhaps to add a sense of realism. Yet analysis of such descriptions often shows that they do not just describe the concrete material environment but also hint at less concrete motives. In "first day" texts, for instance, child safety and child-friendliness are often emphasized, betraying a concern to put school in a favorable light, to legitimize school. Here is an example of safety:

> 5.25  There was a stove with a huge fireguard round it.

And here are some examples of child-friendliness where, again, the point is not to locate exactly where "everything" is but to indicate child-friendly and attractive (or, in the case of critical descriptions, child-unfriendly and unattractive) attributes of the environment and the fixtures in it:

FIGURE 5.9. Visual description (Ladybird, 1977: 7). Illustration from *Talkabout Starting School* by Margaret West and Ethel Wingfield © Ladybird Books, Ltd., 1977. Reproduced by kind permission of Ladybird Books, Ltd.

5.26   Everything is just the right height for Mary Kate.
5.27   It was light with rows of desks and pictures on the walls.
5.28   All around the walls were paintings and drawings and big coloured diagrams and pictures.

This can also be done visually. It is, for example, perfectly possible to *show* the "lightness" indicated in example 5.27, or to use descriptive details, such as pictures

FIGURE 5.10.  Moral evaluation (Leete-Hodge, nd: 36).

on the wall, to convey values, as in figure 5.10, where the picture of the sheep and the lamb perhaps indicates a sense of maternal care.

The inventory in example 5.29 mentions only those spaces that also exist in nursery schools, stressing the familiar and avoiding the new and potentially threatening aspects of the environment:

> 5.29  A reception class contains at least some of the basic elements of the nursery education described above, such as a home corner or a wendy house, a book corner, a carpeted area for floor toys, and, less commonly, trays for sand and water.

Many other descriptions stress authority and hierarchy:

> 5.30  Behind the teacher was a huge blackboard.

In short, descriptions select spaces and spatial elements not only to link them to specific actions and to stress their functionality, or to "interpret space," but also to stress hierarchy and to provide what in chapter 6 I will call "moral evaluation": the use of value-laden adjectives, such as "healthy," "light," "airy," "natural," etc., to trigger moral concepts that can legitimize the practices whose spaces and spatial arrangements are described. The signifiers of such moral evaluations are often relatively marginal to the represented social practices: "decorative" objects, such as pictures on the wall, or nonfunctional qualities of the space, such as "light" and "airy." But the textual salience of these apparently peripheral objects and qualities clearly points at their symbolic importance and their role in getting children (and parents) not just to accept schooling as a fact of life, but also to like it and identify with it. The specific values expressed here, e.g., child-friendliness and a modicum of connection with earlier "preschool" indulgence, are specific to the social institution with which I am concerned here, compulsory education. But elsewhere, description will play the same three general roles of signifying functionality, hierarchy, and moral value, even though the signifiers and the legitimating discourses they invoke will be different.

Visual signifiers can of course fulfill the same functions, as seen, for example, in figure 5.10.

## 5. Subjective and Objective Space

In chapter 4, I discussed the difference between subjective and objective representations of time. A similar distinction can be made in the case of the representation of space. *Subjective space representations* link the space construction to an actor either by means of "relative" circumstances ("to her left," "on his right," "above him," etc.) or by projecting spatial descriptions through perception clauses. There can of course be variants, such as in example 5.33, where the two elements are disjoined and where the second clause is in itself objective, but subjectivized by the (behavioral) perception clause which precedes it:

> 5.31  A long corridor stretched out before them.
> 5.32  Through one of them Mary Kate could see the top of a tree and through the other she could see the church tower.
> 5.33  Mark looked around the room. It was light with rows of desks and pictures on the wall.

The subjective experience of space can also be realized visually, through "point of view" pictures.

## 6. Word and Image

Table 5.1 presents a social practice analysis of excerpts from three texts. All three deal with the same "first day" episode, the telling or reading of a story by the teacher.

You will listen to stories.

Sometimes you will be able to tell stories, too.

FIGURE 5.11. Story telling episode (Taylor, 1988: pp. 36–37). Illustration from *Starting School* by Geraldine Taylor © Ladybird Books, Ltd., 1988. Reproduced by kind permission of Ladybird Books, Ltd.

The first box analyzes the text of example 5.34, the second the text of figure 5.4, and the third the text of figure 5.11. The descriptions of the visuals are italicized.

> 5.34 In the afternoon Miss Laurie read a story to the class, but Mary Kate didn't hear much of it. She was fast asleep on the floor by the doll's house.

Table 5.1 brings out which elements are communicated only visually, which only verbally, and which both visually and verbally. Clearly, in the picture books, only the actions and (some of) the actors are represented verbally. Actors, locations, spatial arrangements, and material resources are all visualized, and so present the concrete elements of the practice in more detail than words alone could have done. In figure 5.11, even the time is visualized. Yet, structurally, the verbal and visual space representations are quite similar. There is a foreground with a teacher on a chair and children on the floor, and a background signifying a setting (a corner with a window, pictures, and drawers; a plant, books, and pictures; a doll's house).

Table 5.2, finally, summarizes the distinctions I have made in this chapter, italicizing those that can be realized both verbally and visually. The only category that

TABLE 5.1.  Three Versions of Storytelling Episode (Social Practice Analysis)

| Actor | Action | Space | Time | Resources |
|---|---|---|---|---|
| teacher | reads story | | in the afternoon | |
| | ~ | | | |
| child | sleeps | on the floor by the doll's house | | |
| *teacher* | *tells the story* reads story ~ | *teacher; on chair; children around teacher on floor; corner with window, picture, and drawers in background* | | book |
| *children* | *listen* | | | |
| *teacher* | *tells story* ~ | *teacher on chair; children in front of teacher on floor; plant, books, and pictures in background* | *2:30 p.m.* | *book, glove puppet* |
| *children*/children | *listen to story/* listen to story ~ | | | |
| *child*/children | *holds puppet/*are able to tell story | | | *glove puppet* |

Note. Descriptions of the visuals are italicized.

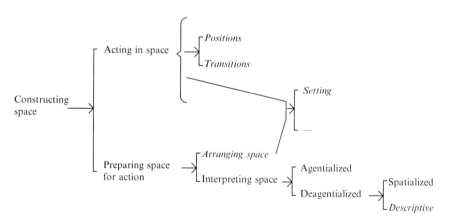

TABLE 5.2.  Space Network

needs words and cannot be realized in both ways is "interpreting space." But this should not be taken as suggesting that images are inferior to words in the range of functions they can fulfill. Clearly, they can present more detail and, as my discussion of figures 5.5 and 5.6 showed, they can indicate the relative position of objects in space much more economically and in much greater detail than is possible with words.

# 6

The Discursive Construction
of Legitimation

**R**econtextualization involves not just the transformation of social practices into discourses about social practices, but also the addition of contextually specific legitimations of these social practices, answers to the spoken or unspoken questions "Why should we do this?" or "Why should we do this in this way?" In this chapter, I set out a framework for analyzing how the answers to such questions are constructed in English discourse.

## 1. Introduction

"Every system of authority attempts to establish and to cultivate the belief in its legitimacy," Max Weber wrote, almost 100 years ago (1977: 325). Language is without doubt the most important vehicle for these attempts. Berger and Luckmann have even argued that, effectively, all of language is legitimation (1966: 112):

> Incipient legitimation is present as soon as a system of linguistic objectification of human experience is transmitted. For example, the transmission of a kinship vocabulary ipso facto legitimates the kinship structure. The fundamental legitimating "explanations" are, so to speak, built into the vocabulary.

In this chapter, I will discuss four major categories of legitimation, in the hope that this will be of use both for critically analyzing the construction of legitimation in discourse and, more generally, for reflection on the problems that face legitimation today:

1. *Authorization*, that is, legitimation by reference to the authority of tradition, custom, law, and/or persons in whom institutional authority of some kind is vested.

2. *Moral evaluation*, that is, legitimation by (often very oblique) reference
   to value systems.
3. *Rationalization*, that is, legitimation by reference to the goals and uses
   of institutionalized social action and to the knowledges that society has
   constructed to endow them with cognitive validity.
4. *Mythopoesis*, that is, legitimation conveyed through narratives whose
   outcomes reward legitimate actions and punish nonlegitimate actions.

These forms of legitimation can occur separately or in combination. They can be
used to legitimize, but also to delegitimize, to critique. They can occupy the largest
part of specific instances of text and talk which may hardly refer to what it is that is
being legitimized, or they can be thinly sprinkled across detailed descriptive or pre-
scriptive accounts of the practices and institutions they legitimize.

## 2. Authorization

If legitimation is the answer to the spoken or unspoken "why" questions—"Why
should we do this?" or "Why should we do this in this way?"—one answer to that
question is "because I say so," where the "I" is someone in whom some kind of
authority is vested, or "because so-and-so says so," where the authority is vested in
"so-and-so." This I will refer to as "personal authorization" or "personal authority
legitimation." The question is: who can exercise this authority, and how?

### (1) Personal Authority

In the case of undiluted personal authority, legitimate authority is vested in people
because of their status or role in a particular institution, e.g., parents and teachers
in the case of children. Such authorities then need not invoke any justification for
what they require others to do other than a mere "because I say so," although in
practice they may of course choose to provide reasons and arguments. Bernstein
(1971: 154) saw personal authority as one of the hallmarks of the "positional family"
in which "judgements are a function of the status of the member" and "disputes are
settled by the relative power inhering in the respective statuses." Not surprisingly, it
is, in my corpus, most commonly associated with children.

Personal authority legitimation typically takes the form of a "verbal process"
clause (Halliday, 1985: 129) in which the "projected clause," the authority's utterance, contains some form of obligation modality, as in this example from one of the
children's stories in my corpus:

> 6.1 Magnus sat down. Because the teacher said they had to.

A specific form of this type of authority is what, in chapter 4, I called the "time summons." Here, it is not so much the activity itself as its timing which is legitimized
through personal authority as, e.g., in

> 6.2 "It's time to go home," she [the mother] said.

(2)  Expert Authority

In the case of expert authority, legitimacy is provided by expertise rather than status. This expertise may be stated explicitly, for instance, by mentioning credentials, but if the expert is well known in the given context, it may be taken for granted, as in certain types of academic discourse which, rather than providing arguments and evidence, quote intellectual megastars, or just add their names in parentheses.

Typically, expert legitimation takes the form of "verbal process clauses" or "mental process clauses" (e.g., Professor so-and-so believes...") with the expert as subject. In multimodal texts, the credentials may be visual, signified by laboratory paraphernalia, books, or other professional attributes. The experts' utterances themselves will carry some kind of recommendation, some kind of assertion that a particular course of action is "best" or "a good idea." No reasons need to be provided, no other answer to the question of "Why should I do this?" than a mere "because Dr. Juan says so." Expert authority may of course be qualified, as in example 6.3 ("some experts," rather than "experts"):

> 6.3  Some experts say it is best to kiss the child, not look back and go.
> 6.4  Dr. Juan believes it may be a good idea to spend some time with the child in class.

In the age of professionalism, expertise has acquired authority in many domains of activity that had previously been the province of families, for instance, child rearing, nutrition, and eventually even sexuality. "In any area where a human need can be imagined," Ivan Illich wrote (1976: 19), "the new professions, dominant, authoritative, monopolistic, legalized—and at the same time debilitating and effectively disabling the individual—have become exclusive experts of the public good." Today, experts increasingly have to surrender their professional autonomy to management structures, and the public is increasingly able to access information that would previously have been jealously guarded by experts. People are also aware of the plurality of expertise, of the fact that many problems have more than one expert solution. As a result, expert authority may be waning, albeit only slowly.

(3)  Role Model Authority

In the case of role model authority, people follow the example of role models or opinion leaders. The role models may be members of a peer group or media celebrities imitated from afar, and the mere fact that these role models adopt a certain kind of behavior, or believe certain things, is enough to legitimize the actions of their followers. Sometimes, "endorsements" are required, as in examples 6.5 and 6.6, where teachers are urged to follow the example of "wise" and "experienced" colleagues. In other contexts, other endorsements would be required, e.g., "cool" or "smart."

> 6.5  The wise teacher finds out the correct way to pronounce the child's name.
> 6.6  Experienced teachers involve the whole class in supporting the newcomer.

Role model authority plays a particularly important role in advertising and lifestyle media. Home decorating magazines, for instance, legitimize their prescriptions ("how to create your own dream home") with stories of the way media personalities or exemplary noncelebrities renovate and decorate their homes ("Penny Minter-Kemp had always wanted to live in a Georgian house, so she set about creating her own look-alike version from a 1950s farmhouse"). As many celebrities are instantly recognizable, role model authority can be conveyed visually, simply by showing celebrities engaged in the actions that are to be legitimized.

The theoretical foundations for the legitimacy of role models were laid in the 1930s, by a then new form of American psychology, symbolic interactionism (Mead, 1934). Symbolic interactionism focused on the way people "take on the attitudes of the groups to which they belong" (ibid.: 33), of the "significant others" in their immediate and their broader cultural environment. After World War II, American popular culture spread the idea of the role model, encouraging young people across the world to take their cues from their peers and from popular culture, rather than from their elders and from tradition. This in turn facilitated the rapid turnover of consumer preferences that has become so vital to the contemporary economy and to the "lifestyle" identities it has fostered.

### (4) Impersonal Authority

Not all authority legitimation is personal. There is also the impersonal authority of laws, rules, and regulations. The answer to the unspoken "why" question is then not "because I say so" or "because Dr. Juan says so" or "because Penny Minter-Kemp does it," but "because the laws (the rules, the policies, the guidelines, etc.) say so." Impersonal authorities can be the subject of verbal process clauses just as readily as can personal authorities ("The rules state . . ."; "The law says . . ."). But the indispensable element in legitimations of this kind is the presence of nouns such as "policy," "regulation," "rule," "law," etc., or their cognate adjectives and adverbs (e.g., "compulsory," "mandatory," "obligatory"), which often appear in impersonal clauses such as:

> 6.7  It is the policy in her area to admit children termly after their fifth birthday.
> 6.8  Playtime is usually a compulsory break in the program.

### (5) The Authority of Tradition

Although the authority of tradition has been declining in many domains, it may still be invoked, particularly through key words like "tradition," "practice," "custom," "habit." Here, the implicit or explicit answer to the "why" question is not "because it is compulsory," but "because this is what we always do" or "because this is what we have always done." It is then assumed that this will, by itself, carry enough weight to go unchallenged:

> 6.9  It was the practice for children in infant schools to be given free milk daily.

However, in the case of tradition, the "why" question is less often asked. The rules of tradition are enforced by everyone, rather than by specific agents: "Each agent has

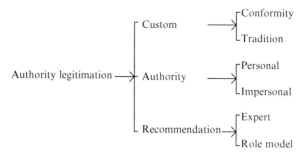

TABLE 6.1. Authority Legitimation

the means of acting as a judge of others and himself," as Bourdieu put it (1977: 17). Everyone has a know-how that is not only experienced as having always existed, but also as not in need of being made explicit or justified.

(6)  The Authority of Conformity

In the case of conformity, finally, the answer to the "why" question is not "because that's what we always do," but "because that's what everybody else does" or "because that's what most people do." The implicit message is, "everybody else is doing it, and so should you" or "most people are doing it, and so should you." No further argument.

Sometimes, conformity legitimation takes the form of an explicit comparison, as in example 6.10:

6.10  Then she let go of Mummy's hand and skipped along towards the open gate of the playground, just as Uncle Jack and Uncle Ned, Auntie Mary and Mummy had done, when they were children.

Most often, however, it is realized through high frequency modality, as in

6.11  The majority of teachers keep records of their progress.
6.12  Many schools now adopt this practice.

In the age of statistics, there is increasing slippage between the rule of law and the rule of conformity. Contemporary lawmakers increasingly believe that, if most people are doing it, it cannot be wrong and should be legalized.

Table 6.1 summarizes the essential categories of authority legitimation.

## 3. Moral Evaluation

Moral evaluation legitimation is based on values, rather than imposed by some kind of authority without further justification. In some cases, moral value is simply asserted by troublesome words such as "good" and "bad," which freely travel among moral, aesthetic, and hedonistic domains and often combine with authority legitimation, as when President George W. Bush legitimizes aggressive policies by pronouncing his enemies an "axis of evil." But in most cases, moral evaluation is linked to specific discourses of moral value. However, these discourses are not made explicit and debatable. They are only hinted at, by means of adjectives such as "healthy," "normal," "natural," "useful," and so on. Such adjectives are then the tip of a submerged iceberg of moral values. They trigger a moral concept, but are detached from the system of interpretation from which they derive, at least on a conscious level. They transmute moral discourses into the kind of "generalized motives" which, as Habermas said (1976: 36), are now "widely used to ensure mass loyalty."

As a result, it is not possible to find an explicit, linguistically motivated method for identifying moral evaluations of this kind. As discourse analysts, we can only "recognize" them, on the basis of our commonsense cultural knowledge. The usefulness of linguistic discourse analysis stops at this point. Historical discourse research has to take over. Only the social and cultural historian can explain the moral status of these expressions, by tracing them back to the moral discourses that underlie them and by undoing the "genesis amnesia" (Bourdieu) that allows us to treat such moral evaluations as commonsense values. In one study (Van Leeuwen and Wodak, 1999), Ruth Wodak and I examined how Viennese magistrates legitimize the refusal of applications from immigrant workers to be reunited with their families by invoking issues of health and hygiene, for instance by arguing that the dwellings of immigrant workers cannot fulfill the "public hygiene conditions" (ibid.: 108) necessary to provide their children with sufficient space for ensuring the "sensible protection of the life environment" that is "beneficial to the educational development of the child."(ibid.: 108) Such concerns originally became legitimate areas of government control in the early twentieth century, for instance in connection with public housing projects and obligatory physical education in schools. At that time, they formed part of a new, social democratic discourse of values that had to be argued for explicitly. Today, they have passed into common sense, even in the legal arguments of Viennese magistrates.

(1) Evaluation

Evaluative adjectives play a key role in moral evaluation legitimation. However, as Leech noted in his study of advertising English (1966), many adjectives are at once "designative" and "attributive." They communicate both concrete qualities of actions or objects and commend them in terms of some domain of values: "praise is mingled with practicality" (ibid.: 130) as, for instance, in the case of favored advertising adjectives such as "green," "crisp," "cool," "golden." This too makes moral evaluation covert and seeks to shield it from debate and argument.

Many of the examples from the "first day at school" corpus use adjectives such as "normal" and "natural" to legitimize the reactions of parents. These adjectives then modify either a nominal group which has a nominalized reference to a practice (or one or more of its constituent actions or reactions) as its head (as in "a natural and healthy response"), or an attribute in a relational clause which has the practice (or a constituent action or reaction) as its subject (as in "being upset is natural"):

6.13  It is perfectly normal to be anxious about starting school.
6.14  It is only natural that the first days of school are upsetting.
6.15  Showing signs of stress about starting school is a natural and healthy response.

In other words, do not take your distress as signaling that what happens here is not right, not legitimate. It is "normal," "natural," "healthy."

"Naturalization" legitimation may also be achieved by reference to time or to the concept of "change." This occurs particularly often in children's books, as in examples 6.16 and 6.17:

6.16  Soon Autumn would be here and Mark and Mandy would have to start school.
6.17  Mary Kate was five. She had been five for a whole week and tomorrow she would be going to school.

At which age or in which month children start school is a matter of the policies of education authorities and differs from authority to authority. But to the child, it is represented here as a life change that is just as impossible to stop as the rhythm of day and night or of the seasons. "Naturalization" is a specific form of moral evaluation, a form which in fact denies morality and replaces moral and cultural orders with the "natural order." Morality and nature become entangled here, and discourse analytical methods cannot disentangle them. The only criterion for distinguishing between a true natural order and a moral and cultural order disguising itself as a natural order is the question of whether we are dealing with something that can, in principle, be changed by human intervention. And that is not always an easy question to answer.

## (2)  Abstraction

Another way of expressing moral evaluations is by referring to practices (or to one or more of their component actions or reactions) in abstract ways that "moralize" them by distilling from them a quality that links them to discourses of moral values. Instead of "the child goes to school for the first time," we might say "the child takes up independence," so that the practice of schooling is legitimized in terms of a discourse of "independence." Instead of "playing in the playground," we might say "get along with others" or "cooperate," which legitimizes the opportunities for playing which the school creates in terms of a discourse of "sociability." Instead of "attending parents' nights," we might say "build up a relationship with the school" or "be involved with the school"—abstractions which foreground desired and legitimate qualities of cooperation, engagement, and commitment.

## (3)  Analogies

Another common method of expressing moral evaluation is the analogy: comparisons in discourse almost always have a legitimating or delegitimating function. Here, the implicit answer to the question "Why must I do this?" or "Why must I do this in this way?" is not "because it is good," but "because it is like another activity which is associated with positive values" (or, in the case of negative comparison, "because it is not like another activity which is associated with negative values"). Sometimes, the comparison is implicit. An activity that belongs to one social practice is described by a term which, literally, refers to an activity belonging to another social practice, and the positive or negative values which, in the given sociocultural context, are attached to that other activity are then transferred to the original activity. Ivan Illich, in his critique of schooling (1971), for instance, imports terms from the military, the prison, etc., to refer to the actions of teachers and speaks of "drilling pupils," "incarcerating pupils," and so on.

Comparisons can also be expressed explicitly, through similarity conjunction or circumstances of comparison:

> 6.18  Like an adult starting in a new job...the child will be worried.
> 6.19  It will become as automatic as cleaning your teeth.

In example 6.20, the comparison is narrativized. Schooling is compared to maternal care through reference to a picture of a "sheep and her lambs" on the wall. Needless to say, this comparison may invoke an ambiguous set of other cultural references as well, as sheep are a major source of comparisons in the Bible:

> 6.20  The room was light with rows of desks just like his, and pictures on the walls. One showed a big sheep and her lambs. He liked that, but the map did not look very interesting.

My final two examples extend comparisons across a stretch of discourse—the first in order to legitimize, the second in order to delegitimize schooling:

> 6.21  When a seedling is transplanted from one place to another, the transplantation may be a stimulus or a shock. The careful gardener seeks to minimize shock, so that the plant is re-established as quickly as possible. Similarly, for the child moving from one provision to another, a smooth transition requires that the change is sufficient to be stimulating but not so drastic as to cause shock.
> 6.22  Children are protected by neither the First nor the Fifth Amendment when they stand before that secular priest, the teacher. The child must confront a man [sic] who wears an invisible triple crown, like a papal tiara. The symbol of triple authority combines in one person for the child, the teacher pontificates as pastor, prophet and priest—he is at once guide, teacher and administrator of a sacred ritual.

Table 6.2 summarizes the essential categories of moral evaluation.

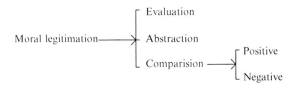

TABLE 6.2.  Moral Evaluation Legitimation

## 4. Rationalization

In contemporary discourse, moralization and rationalization keep each other at arm's length. In the case of moral evaluation, rationality has gone underground. And as we will see in this section, in the case of rationalization, morality remains oblique and submerged, even though no rationalization can function as legitimation without it.

I will distinguish two main types of rationality. *Instrumental rationality* legitimizes practices by reference to their goals, uses, and effects. *Theoretical rationality* legitimizes practices by reference to a natural order of things, but much more explicitly than the kinds of naturalization I discussed earlier.

### (1) Instrumental Rationalization

Like legitimations, purposes are constructed in discourse in order to explain why social practices exist, and why they take the forms they do. What is the purpose of going to school? And what is the purpose of giving schooling the form it takes in our society? The question is: are all purposes also legitimations? I believe not. In order to serve as legitimations, purpose constructions must contain an element of moralization, in the sense in which I described it in the previous section. Only this can turn purposes and purposiveness into what Habermas (1976: 22) called a "strategic-utilitarian morality."

Departing from Weber's account of the way modern Western society has made science, morality, and art into distinct domains, Habermas characterizes the institutions that regulate different kinds of social action in terms of the validity claims, or "kinds of truth" which underlie and legitimize them. Thus, "teleological action," the category with which I am concerned in this section, is founded on the principle of success, of "whether it works or not," i.e., on a rationality of means and ends. "Conversation" is founded on the criterion of truth, of whether an action truthfully represents states of affairs in the objective world. "Norm-conformative action" is founded on the principle of right and wrong, on whether an action is morally justified. And "dramaturgical action" is founded on the principle of honesty, of whether the action is sincere and whether the actor is truthful to his or her feelings.

Focusing on "teleological action," consider the following examples:

6.23  His mother joins the queue to pay his dinner money to the teacher.

6.24  The reception teachers went to the nursery unit to see their prospective pupils.

6.25  Mary Kate went upstairs after breakfast to have another look at them [i.e., her new school satchel, pinny, etc.].

6.26  Jane's teacher used eye contact and facial expression to establish positive bonds with her.

6.27  The following strategies were employed to make the introduction to PE more smooth.

6.28  The children use specific apparatus and movements to promote muscular coordination and agility.

All of the examples contain the same three basic elements: an activity ("going upstairs," "using apparatus," etc.), a purpose link (the preposition "to"), and the purpose itself, which may either be another activity or a state (e.g., "have another look," "make smooth"). But in the first three examples (6.23–6.25), the purpose is a *generalized action*. The actions inside the purpose clause are the kind of straightforward generalized representations of actions that could serve as labels for whole activity sequences and form what Roland Barthes (1977) called the "nuclei" of activity sequences. The other actions, the more "micro-actions" whose purposefulness is established in the text, are purposeful *in relation to* these nuclei, as parts of the whole, necessary preparations for the nuclear activity, and so on. "Joining the queue," for instance, is a component action of an activity sequence of which "paying dinner money to the teacher" is the nucleus and main purpose. As a result, the whole of the sequence can be called "paying dinner money to the teacher." In the second three examples (6.26–6.28), the process inside the purpose clause is a *moralized action* in the sense in which I have described it above, an expression which refers to an action by distilling from it a quality (such as "agile" or "smooth") which can "moralize" it, link it to a discourse of values. "Smooth," for instance, connotes a discourse of efficiency, in which actions, to be legitimate, must unfold in an orderly manner, without friction, without hitches, without disturbances.

All of this applies of course also to the idea of purpose itself. Expressions like "it is useful," "it is effective," and so on are themselves legitimating, descendants of philosophical traditions such as utilitarianism and pragmatism, which explicitly argued for purposefulness, usefulness, and effectiveness as criteria of truth and foundations for norm-conformative, ethical behavior.

Given these preambles, a number of different types of instrumentality can be distinguished. In the case of *goal orientation*, purposes are constructed as "in people," as conscious or unconscious motives, aims, intentions, goals, etc. This requires (a) that the agency of the purposeful actor is explicitly expressed, and (b) that the purposeful action and the purpose have the same agent or, if the purpose is a state, that the person to whom that state is attributed is also the agent of the purposeful action, in other words, the formula is "I do *x* in order to do (or be, or have) *y*." This can then be realized explicitly, by a purpose clause with "to," "in order to," "so as to," etc., as in example 6.29, or remain implicit, as in example 6.30:

6.29 Jane's teacher used eye contact and facial expression to establish positive bonds with her.
6.30 Your child may respond by spending hours happily entertaining herself drawing while she develops her visual, creative and motor skills.

The difference between the two types of realization is significant. Generally, the greater the power of a particular role in a social practice, the more often the agents who fulfill that role will be represented as intentional, as people who can decide to act on the world and succeed in this.

In the case of *means orientation*, the purpose is constructed as "in the action," and the action as a means to an end. The formula is then either "I achieve doing (or being, or having) *y* by *x*-ing," which leaves the agency intact and uses circumstances of means with "by," "by means of," "through," etc., or "*x*-ing serves to achieve being (or doing, or having) *y*," which does not. Two examples of each:

6.31 Children cope with these difficulties by keeping the two worlds apart and never talking about home at school or mentioning school at home.

6.32 The skillful teacher can save the new entrant's face by showing herself to be on his side.

6.33 Formal group time is a powerful mechanism for social control.

6.34 The key to a smooth transition lies in avoiding the shock of anything sudden in the way of sights, sounds or experiences.

A number of subcategories are described in Van Leeuwen (2000a), for instance, the category of *use*, where the purposeful action is represented as a tool to achieve a goal:

6.35 Registration can also be used to encourage children to respond to their own names and learn each others'.

Another subcategory focuses on the *potential* of specific actions for serving specific purposes and uses clauses with "facilitating" processes, such as "allow," "promote," "help," "teach," "build," "facilitate," etc., in which the purposeful action is subject and the purpose object or complement, for instance:

6.36 It helps her to develop her sense of time.

Effect orientation, finally, stresses the outcome of actions. Here, purposefulness is looked at from the other end, as something that turned out to exist in hindsight, rather than as something that was, or could have been, planned beforehand. Those involved might be able to predict the outcome, but they cannot fully bring it about through their own actions. In this case, there is no identity between the agent of the action, whose purpose is to be constructed, and the agent of the action that constitutes the purpose itself. Instead of a goal, as in example 6.37, or a means, as in 6.38, the purpose is the outcome of an action, as in example 6.39. Typically, this is expressed by result clauses with "so that," "that way," etc.

6.37 Your child has to learn to control aggressiveness, so as to be accepted by others.

6.38 Your child will be accepted by others by learning to control aggressiveness.

6.39 Your child has to learn to control aggressiveness, so others accept him.

In a second subcategory, the case of *effect*, the purposeful action itself is the agent or initiator of the purpose action:

6.40 Sending children away from home at an early age builds character.

6.41 Establishing the same routine going to and from school will make your child feel secure.

## (2) Theoretical Rationalization

In the case of theoretical rationalization, legitimation is grounded not in whether the action is morally justified or not, nor in whether it is purposeful or effective, but in whether it is founded on some kind of truth, on "the way things are." Theoretical rationalization is therefore closely related to the category of naturalization, which I discussed earlier. But where naturalizations simply state that some practice or action is "natural," theoretical legitimations provide explicit representations of "the way things are."

Typically, theoretical legitimation takes one of three forms. The first is that of the *definition*, in which one activity is defined in terms of another, moralized activity. For a definition to be a definition, both activities must be objectivated and generalized, and the link between them must either be attributive ("is," "constitutes," etc.) or significative ("means," "signals," "symbolizes," etc.). In the examples below, "necessary" hints at a utilitarian and "growing up" at an adult, "reality principle"–oriented discourse of values.

> 6.42  Transition is a necessary stage in the young child's experience.
> 6.43  School signals that her children are growing up.

Such statements function either as a kind of axiom, referring forward to the more detailed activities to which they are hyponymically related, or as a conclusion, referring backward to the activities they summarize.

In the case of the *explanation*, it is not the practice which is defined or characterized, but one or more of the actors involved in the practice. Here the answer to the "why" question is: "because doing things this way is appropriate to the nature of these actors." Generality is again essential. Explanations describe general attributes or habitual activities of the categories of actors in question. In the case of the "first day at school," many of the parents' activities are legitimized by reference to lay or expert forms of child psychology. Parents use the same route to school each day because "small children thrive on routine." They stay calm and composed because "children read their parents' distress so readily."

A final form of theoretical legitimation takes the form of *predictions*. Although predictions have a ring of authority about them, they are meant to be based not on authority, but on expertise, and they can therefore be denied by contrary experience, at least in principle. An example:

> 6.44  Don't worry if you or your child cries. It won't last long.

Berger and Luckmann distinguished between "experiential" and "scientific" rationalizations. They described *experiential rationalizations* as "various explanatory schemes relating sets of objective meanings," and they added that "these schemes are highly pragmatic, directly related to concrete actions" and that "proverbs, moral maxims and wise sayings are common on this level" (Berger and Luckmann, 1966: 112). Like moral evaluations, they function as commonsense knowledge, regardless of whether they originate in theoretical rationalizations or not, but they are more explicitly formulated, and therefore more open to debate, albeit in experiential and anecdotal, rather than in scientific terms.

*Scientific rationalizations* are the "differentiated bodies of knowledge" that are developed to legitimate specific institutions. They not only include modern science but also other systematic bodies of knowledge that are used to legitimize institutional practices, for instance, religions:

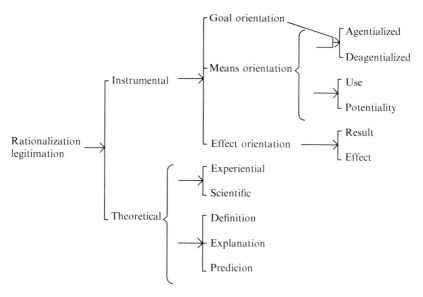

TABLE 6.3.  Rationalization Legitimation

> Such legitimations form fairly comprehensive frames of reference for the respective
> sectors of institutionalised conduct. Because of their complexity and differentiation
> they are frequently entrusted to specialised personnel who transmit them through
> formalised initiation procedures. (Berger and Luckmann, 1966: 112)

As my examples have shown, psychology is, today, one of these specialized
institutions for the production of discourses that can "explain" the nature of social
actors and legitimize social practices, one of the institutions that inform the "changing popular syntheses of isolated items of scientific information" (Habermas, 1976:
80) used by the media and other forms of public communication to legitimize a
range of social practices. Because of this mediation, psychologists and other cre-
ators of legitimating discourses can remain at arm's length from the legitimating uses
of their work, and often it is only in hindsight that the connections between scientific discourses and institutionalized social practices can be clearly perceived as, for
instance, in the case of the now-discredited forms of anthropology that were used to
legitimize the institutionalization of colonial practices.

Table 6.3 summarizes the essential categories of rationalization legitimation.

## 5. Mythopoesis

Legitimation can also be achieved through storytelling. In *moral tales*, protagonists
are rewarded for engaging in legitimate social practices or restoring the legitimate
order. In stories about going to school for the first time, for instance, children must
face the trauma of leaving the security of home, but then, after negotiating a number

of obstacles, they overcome this trauma and experience a happy ending of one kind
or another:

6.45 "It-was-such-fun-we-had-milk-and-I-knew-a-bird," gasped Mandy all in one
     breath.
         "Yes, I enjoyed it too," said Mark as they walked home telling of all that happened
     at their first day at school. They would always remember it.
6.46 No wonder there had been so many voices cheering her on. The whole family had
     come with Daddy to see Mary Kate win her first race.

*Cautionary tales*, on the other hand, convey what will happen if you do not conform to the norms of social practices. Their protagonists engage in deviant activities
that lead to unhappy endings.

In most of the stories I have quoted, "going to school for the first time" is represented in a fairly straightforward way, but in many other stories the actors and/or
actions are inverted in terms of specific semantic features. A common inversion in
"going to school for the first time" stories is the inversion of the semantic feature
"human." A striking example occurs in one of the children's books I studied. The
children are in the classroom for the first time and the first lesson begins with the
teacher holding up pictures of animals and the children responding (Leete-Hodge,
n.d.: 39–40):

6.47 Miss Carter held up some large coloured pictures of animals. "Cat," "dog," "horse,"
     shouted the children as they recognised the animals. "Bird," yelled Mandy as she
     saw a sparrow appear. "Good," said Miss Carter, "now what about this one?" and she
     held up a picture of a funny looking brown animal in a cage.
         "A monkey," called one little boy who remembered seeing a monkey cry when he
     had been taken to the zoo for his holiday treat. "The poor thing could not reach for
     a nut that someone had thrown him!"

The story of the "first day at school" is here interrupted by another, embedded one,
a brief story of a visit to the zoo and of a monkey who was unable to pick up the
nut that "someone had thrown him." This was not the only time in my research that
animals appeared in what were otherwise straightforward accounts of "the first day."
There were dogs who were not allowed inside and could not understand why, and
there were children taking animals into the classroom, which then resulted in may-
hem of one kind or another:

6.48 The teacher wrote the name down in the register: NOIL. Then she finished calling
     the register.
         "Betty Small," she said.
         "Yes," said the little girl.
         "Noil," said the teacher.
         "Yes," said the lion. He mumbled, opening his mouth as little as possible so that the
     teacher should not see his teeth as sharp as skewers and knives. He did not swish his
     tail. He did not growl. He sat next to the little girl, as good as gold.

TABLE 6.4. Mythopoesis

Schooling is represented here as the transition from an animal-like to a truly human state. This is an old theme. In *The History of Animals*, Aristotle (2004) wrote that young children differ little from animals. By going to school, these stories suggest, children transcend their animal-like state. Compulsory schooling is legitimized as an evolutionary and, in the case of the lion, also a civilizing process. The child moves from being at one with animals to a higher stage, where animals cannot follow, and the animal's failure to understand, or to comply with the rules of school, confirms this. As in the stories of many other cultures, "the diversity of species is used as a conceptual support for social differentiation" (Lévi-Strauss, 1967: 174).

Stories may also use symbolic actions, specific actions that can nevertheless represent more than one domain of institutionalized social practice and so provide a "mythical model of social action" (Wright, 1975: 188). We have already encountered the story of Magnus and the Unknown Soldier (Van Leeuwen, 1981). In the story, these two end up in a room where adults are sitting on benches, and where the "man with the large mustache" orders them to complete a series of tests. The Unknown Soldier fails miserably at this task and Magnus is not allowed to help him. In the end, Magnus is told to leave and, despite vigorous protest, must leave his friend the Unknown Soldier behind. Clearly this story represents not just schooling, but all domains where anonymous people are compelled to spend their days locked up in rooms, engaged in meaningless tasks, and in which they must forgo solidarity and compete with each other, so that some may succeed and others fail. Just as fairy tales distance their readers from the actuality of their subject matter in faraway places and long-ago times, so this story distances its readers from the naturalistic specifics of institutions such as the army, the factory, the office, and the school, to allow the delegitimation of all of these domains and of the principles of social organization that underlie them.

Table 6.4 summarizes the key categories of mythopoesis.

## 6. Multimodal Legitimation

Though language plays the central role in legitimation, some forms of legitimation can also be expressed visually, or even musically. Stories, for instance, can be told visually, in the form of comic strips, movies, and games. Role models can be shown as engaged in actions that need legitimation. And moral evaluations

Daniel shows Anna
where to hang her coat.

FIGURE 6.1.  Daniel shows Anna where to hang her coat.
Reproduced by permission of Althea Braithwaite.

can be connoted visually or represented by visual symbols. Figure 6.1 depicts an episode that occurs in almost all "going to school for the first time" children's stories: the "coat-rack episode." This episode is often used to portray the child's initial dismay at finding herself one among many, rather than a unique individual. For this reason, the coat hooks are often individualized with the child's name or with her own, personal picture. In figure 6.1, an element is added to the basic representation of the episode, the teddy bear in the left bottom corner. The psychoanalyst D. W. Winnicott (1971: 2) has described teddy bears as "transitional objects" to which the child transfers affection as she moves from a stage of "oral eroticism" into a "growing ability to recognise and accept reality." As a result, teddy bears have come to symbolize affection in a wide range of contexts (Caldas-Coulthard and Van Leeuwen, 2003) and can legitimize schooling by suggesting that school is not an impersonal and depersonalizing institution, but allows at least a modicum of affection and a small acknowledgment of the child's "oral erotic" past.

In a brochure for parents, a young girl poses in her new uniform, a little anxiously, perhaps. The strong presence of a well-lit, large fern in the background adds a hint of the "natural" and of the idea of "growth" to the regimental connotations of the uniform.

In audiovisual texts, music may accompany the representation of social practices, and this too can add moral evaluation legitimation. The film *Blackhawk Down* (Ridley Scott, 2002) opens with a scene, shot in bluish monochrome, of a man wrapping a corpse. The scene is intercut with title cards telling the story of the Somalian famine of 1992 and explaining its causes. The scene is accompanied by a musical lament mingled with the sound of wind. The final title reads: "In late August, America's elite soldiers, Delta Force, Army Rangers and the 160th SOAR are sent to Mogadishu to remove Aidid and restore order." At this point, the sound of a helicopter mixes with the melancholy music, and soon the music becomes energetic, optimistic in its tonality, and militaristic in its instrumentation. Thus, images of the famine are accompanied by a musical discourse of victimhood, and images of the arrival of the American troops by music with heroic connotations.

## 7. Legitimation and Context

Gunther Kress's analysis (1985a: 15–17) of a speech by Helen Caldicott at a large antinuclear rally in Sydney, Australia, powerfully demonstrates the contemporary proliferation of legitimation discourses. He shows that a single text can invoke many different, sometimes even contradictory, discourses: "medical, Christian, populist, (Jungian) psychiatric, patriotic, sentimental/parental, romantic, patriarchal, technological, prophetic, feminist" (ibid.: 17):

> The traces of these different discourses are evident enough; they have not been closely integrated by the writer/speaker into anything like a seamless text: the discursive differences are not resolved. Consequently the text is unlikely to provide that definitional impulse which would act to give unity to the diverse groups which had assembled that day to hear this speech. Although the text is that of a single writer the contention of the different discourses is clearly evident, so much so in fact that it has been beyond the writer's ability to control that difference. (ibid.)

Viewing these discourses as legitimation discourses can add a further dimension, as the concept of legitimation can link social practices with discourses of value. Consider, for instance, the "patriotic" segment of Caldicott's speech:

> 6.49  Thank you, thank you fellow Australians. You're a great country. [loud clapping and shouts] This is the best country in the world. [clapping] And that's why we have an enormous responsibility because we have to lead the earth to survival, and it's Australia that started it fourteen years ago with the French tests. It was us who took the lead to take the French to the Court of Justice at The Hague, to discipline her. And now she tests underground, and it was marches like this that stopped the French blowing up bombs in the Pacific. When I tell the Americans what the Australians did about the French tests they all stand up and cheer. [clapping, yells]

A legitimation analysis of this segment will, on the one hand separate out the actors, actions, and so on from the reactions, purposes, and legitimations but, on the other hand, also show how these two aspects of the text, the representations and the interpretations, one could say, are related. In table 6.5, this is done by aligning the legitimations with the actions and/or actors they legitimize.

TABLE 6.5. Social Practice Analysis of Excerpt 1 from Antinuclear Speech by Helen Caldicott

| Actors | Actions | Reactions | Purposes | Legitimations |
|---|---|---|---|---|
| the French | below up bombs in the Pacific | | | |
| | ↓ | | | |
| the Australians | take the French to the Court of Justice in The Hague | | to discipline them | evaluations of "Australians": *great, best in the world, fantastic people* |
| | ~ | | | |
| the Australians | stopped French by marching | | | moralized activities: *have responsibility, lead earth to survival* |
| | ↓ | | | |
| the French | test underground | | | |
| the Americans | | cheer | | |

The left-hand columns of the grid reconstruct the activity sequence that underlies the text, though agency and sequence are not entirely clear: have the French been stopped by the marching, by the court in The Hague, or both? And in which order did these events occur? The right-hand column shows the legitimations, which, as Kress notes, are quite diverse, even in this short segment: patriotic values are invoked as well as "responsibility" and "survival" discourses.

In a second excerpt from the Caldicott speech, the discourses are perhaps, in Kress's terms, "prophetic," "romantic," and "sentimental/parental":

6.50 Will man evolve spiritually and emotionally enough...and women, to know that we can't fight and we have to live together in peace[?] If we can't we'll blow up the world and you and I will know that in our lifetime. Before we die, we will know whether the human race can do it or not. If we die in a nuclear holocaust, we'll know we failed. If we die of natural causes in our lifetime, we'll definitely know that we succeeded. You can do nothing [more] with your life than this...to give everything up for the planet. And even if you fail, as the bomb goes off, you can die with a clear conscience. But it makes the earth so precious and I really and truly believe that the people of the earth are rising up and the politicians will have to stand aside and give us what we want. We want the earth to continue and we want to live; and have children and life to go on for evermore.

The "prophetic" element is contained in the activity sequence itself (see table 6.6), as it unfolds two scenarios for the future, a doom scenario, in which "we'll blow up the world," and a scenario of hope, in which the politicians will "stand aside." The discourses that legitimize the scenario of hope again vary: discourses of sacrifice and

TABLE 6.6. Social Practice Analysis of Excerpt 2 from Antinuclear Speech by Helen Caldicott

| Actors | Actions | | Legitimations |
|---|---|---|---|
| the human race/we | protest against nuclear arms | | moralized activities: *give everything for the planet, evolve spiritually and emotionally* (discourse of sacrifice?) |
| politicians | blow up the world ↓ | stand aside & disarm ↓ | |
| | die | live in peace have children | *clear conscience* |
| the human race/we | | ↓ | |
| | | die of natural causes | moralized activities: *the earth continues: life goes on for evermore* |

"conscience" mix with discourses in which "life," "the human race," and "the earth" are the ultimate values.

Clearly, it is true, as Kress writes, that "the discursive differences are not resolved" and that, in terms of these discourses, "the text is unlikely to provide that definitional impulse which would act to give unity to the diverse groups which had assembled that day" (Kress, 1985a: 17). We are divided in terms of discourse and, as a result, legitimation, insofar as it is grounded, however obliquely, in moral discourses rather than in authority, is in crisis. On the other hand, the participants in this rally, discursively divided as they may have been, were united in what they were actually doing. They all participated in the same practice: attending the rally and demonstrating against nuclear arms.

Does this provide a starting point for a new, common morality, a morality centered on actions rather than beliefs? Or does it signal a devaluation of beliefs, turning ideas, moral or otherwise, into products on the supermarket shelf, essentially identical, but differently branded so as to allow consumers to express their lifestyle identities and marketers to sell their products as widely as possible? Whatever may be the case, it is clear that in the matter of legitimation we face a choice between morality and authority. And it is equally clear that in reflecting on the crisis of legitimation, we need to consider not just legitimation, but also and especially the intricate interconnections between social practices and the discourses that legitimize them.

# The Discursive Construction
# of Purpose

In this chapter, I set out a framework for analyzing how the purposes of social practices are constructed, interpreted, and negotiated in English discourse. I then apply the framework to an analysis of examples drawn, again, from my "first day at school" corpus of texts.

## 1. Introduction

In this chapter, I do not offer a theory of the purpose(s) of discourse. I do not even take a position on whether discourses are, in some absolute sense, purposeful or not. My topic is the discursive *construction* of the purposes of social practices (including discursive practices). I take the view that social action (again, including discursive action) is not inherently purposeful or, at least, we cannot prove that it is. The same action may be constructed in one context as oriented toward a specific goal; in another as performed not to achieve a particular purpose, but out of tradition (because it is "the done thing"); in yet another as performed for the sake of the intrinsic satisfaction it provides (because "I like doing it"). Even when a given action is constructed as purposeful, different purposes may be ascribed to it in different social contexts. An advertiser may see the promotion of goods and services as the purpose of advertising, a left-wing social critic, the promulgation of consumerist values, a postmodern cultural theorist, the celebration of irony and wit. Who is right? One thing is certain, the construction of purpose is often at the heart of disagreement and conflict.

The construction of social action as purposeful and the construction and negotiation of specific purposes for specific social actions are not equally important in every domain of discourse. Where social action is governed by tradition, or where affective and aesthetic satisfaction determine what is done and how it is done, the discursive construction of purpose will take a back seat. But where new things are to be done, or where old things are to be done in new ways, purpose will be paramount, for instance, in instructional texts, syllabuses, or strategic planning documents with their ritual foregrounding of the aims and objectives of the actions they propose.

## 2. Purpose and Legitimation

In chapter 6, I touched on the relation between purpose and legitimation. The discursive construction of purpose is closely related, but not identical, to the discursive construction of legitimation. Like purpose, legitimation is not inherent in action, but discursively constructed, in order to explain why social practices exist and why they take the forms they do—why, for instance, children must go to school, and why schooling takes place the way it does in our society. This question always lurks in the background, even if it is not explicitly asked, especially, as Berger and Luckmann (1966) have pointed out, in relation to social practices, conventions, rules, and laws in whose genesis we have not ourselves played a role and whose historical raison d'être is therefore not part of our own memory. In the case of *purpose legitimation*, the answer to that question is couched in terms of purposes, by saying, for instance, that children have to go to school "in order to learn to read and write" or "to develop their creative, conceptual, and motor skills."

The question arises: are all purposes legitimations? And if so, why make "purpose" a separate category? The answer I give is no; in order to serve as legitimations, an additional feature is required. They must, as Habermas puts it (1976: 22), make "submerged and oblique reference to moral values in a frame of instrumentality, to achieve a 'strategic-utilitarian morality.' "

It is possible to distinguish between legitimating and nonlegitimating purpose constructions. In example 7.1, for instance, the action in the purpose construction ("pay dinner money") is a *generalized action*, and the action whose purpose is being constructed ("join the queue") is one of the "micro-actions" that make up the "pay dinner money" episode and take their meaning from it. The same applies to 7.2: "going to the nursery unit" is part of the broader action of "seeing their prospective pupils" and takes its meaning from that broader action:

7.1  His mother joins the queue to pay his dinner money to the teacher.
7.2  The reception teachers went to the nursery unit to see their prospective pupils.

In 7.3 and 7.4, on the other hand, the actions in the purpose clauses are moralized actions, ways of referring to particular actions that connote moral values:

7.3  The following strategies were employed to make the introduction to PE more smooth.
7.4  The children used specific apparatus and movements to promote muscular coordination and agility.

*Moralized actions* are realized not by means of generalizations, but by means of abstractions, of expressions which distill, from the actions to which they refer, particular, often seemingly peripheral aspects or qualities, such as, for instance "smoothness" or "agility." The expression "make the introduction smooth" in 7.3 does refer, in the context, to what the teacher actually does. But it does so in a peculiarly abstract way to highlight a quality ("smoothness") which can then be used to legitimize the "strategies" referred to. Such qualities are evidently not unique to the actions that are represented here. There are many other transitions which can be made "smooth" and many other contexts in which "muscular coordination and agility" can be promoted. They are also *moral* qualities, because they trigger intertextual references to the discourses of moral values that underpin them: "smooth," for instance, connotes a discourse of efficiency, in which action must unfold in an orderly manner, without friction, without hitches, without disturbances. "Promote muscular coordination and agility" invokes discourses of the beautiful and healthy body. Even in these discourses, however, the moral values are rarely made explicit. Their origins and histories remain, as Habermas says, submerged. They are only obliquely referred to, only connoted through the abstract representations of actions I have described. They are treated as common sense and do not make explicit the religious and philosophical traditions from which they ultimately draw their values and on which their legitimating capacity ultimately rests. This also applies to the idea of purpose itself. Expressions like "it is purposeful," "it is useful," "it is effective," and so on are themselves legitimating, descendants of philosophical traditions such as utilitarianism and pragmatism, which explicitly argued for purposefulness, usefulness, and effectiveness as criteria of truth and foundations for ethical behavior.

## 3. The Grammar of Purpose

In this section, I will discuss the principal types of purpose which can be realized in English and the ways in which they are realized. It follows from the preceding section that all of the constructions I will discuss may either be legitimating (as realized by the presence of moralized actions in the purpose construction) or not.

As was made evident in section 2, three elements are necessary for the discursive construction of purposeful action: (a) the *purposeful action*, that is, the action whose purpose is to be constructed (e.g., the action "using specific apparatus and movements" in example 7.4); (b) the *purpose*, itself a process, an action, or a state (e.g., the action "promoting muscular coordination and agility" in the same example), and (c) the *purpose link*, the relation of purposefulness between these two (e.g., the nonfinite clause with "to," again in example 7.4). As with other semantic relations, the relation of purposefulness may be explicit or implicit (Martin, 1992: 183–84). Explicit relations will be expressed either by some form of conjunction or by a logical process, in this case, a "purpose process," such as "serves to," "aims to," or some kind of metaphorical equivalent. In the case of implicit realizations, the clause expressing the purpose will not be explicitly coded as a purpose clause. Instead of a purpose conjunction, there may, for instance, be a temporal conjunction (simultaneity) or an explanatory conjunction. There is, however, an *implicit* purpose conjunction, and it can be demonstrated by inserting a purpose link or by replacing the existing temporal or explanatory link with a purpose link. When this is possible, there is an implicit purpose construction; when it is not, there is not. In example 7.5, for instance, it is possible to insert a purpose link. It makes sense to change 7.5 into "One or two teachers took the new entrants on a tour of the school, to show them where everything was and to introduce them to key figures on the way." The same cannot be done with example 7.6. It does not make sense to change that example into "'Does Mandy Williams live here?' asked the man to raise his peaked cap":

> 7.5   One or two teachers took the new entrants on a tour of the school. She showed them where everything was and introduced them to key figures on the way.
> 7.6   "Does Mandy Williams live here?" asked the man raising his peaked cap.

## (1) Goal-Oriented Action

I already touched on this category in the previous chapter, where I wrote that some purpose constructions "construct purposes as 'in people,' as conscious or unconscious motives, aims, intentions, goals, etc." The agency of the actor of the purposeful action should be explicitly realized and the action is 'activated' (Van Leeuwen, 1995) by being expressed as a finite or nonfinite clause. The purposeful action and the purpose should have the same agent. If the purpose is a state, the person to whom the state is attributed should also be the agent of the purposeful action. As I said in the previous chapter, 'the essential meaning of this type of purpose construction can be formulated as "I do x in order to do (or be, or have) y"—which can then either be made explicit by a purpose clause with "to," "in order to," "so as to," etc. (examples 7.7–7.9) or remain implicit (examples 7.10–7.12).

> 7.7   Mummy and Mary Kate went upstairs to get dressed.
> 7.8   Some teachers come in before the term starts to prepare an attractive setting for the children.
> 7.9   Mothers take their tots to baby clinics to check their health.
> 7.10  Some head teachers gave talks to parents at local playgroups, giving hints on how best to help the child.
> 7.11  The children go a few at a time to the class shop and buy a bottle of milk with toy money.
> 7.12  Your child may respond by spending hours happily entertaining herself drawing, while she develops her visual, creative and motor skills.

Social actors whose actions are *explicitly* constructed as purposeful in this way are discursively empowered as intentional agents—as people who can decide to, and then succeed in, changing the world, whether in minor or major ways, or as people who can set a goal and then determine, autonomously, how to achieve it. *Implicit* realizations retain the agency, but as the intentionality is not explicitly expressed, it can be denied. It remains open to interpretation. It is left to the listener or reader whether to interpret the link between action and purpose as intentional or not.

A specific kind of goal-oriented purpose construction is the *precaution*. Here, it is the purpose of the action to *prevent* something from happening or from being done. This is realized by means of a hypotactic clause with "in case" or "because otherwise," or with a negative result clause ("so that... not"):

> 7.13 "Here are some biscuits to put in your satchel," said Granny, "in case you feel peckish when you have your mid-morning milk."
> 7.14 "That's what we'll call you then. That way we shan't muddle you up with the other Mary."

Another specific kind of goal-oriented purpose construction is the *preparation*, where it is the purpose of the action to be prepared for something rather than actually do it. This is realized by clauses with "ready for" or "ready to," e.g.:

> 7.15 Mummy had put all her things on the little blue dressing-table, ready for the morning.
> 7.16 She could see her party dress hanging up, ready to wear when it was time to dress.

Other specific types of goal-oriented purposeful action may exist, although I have not found any in my data. An example would be the subjective coding of purposes in terms of desire, or other related mental processes ("I do *x* because I want *y*"). There were, however, no instances of this in my data.

## (2) Means-Oriented Action

Purpose construction may also construct purpose as "in the action." In this case, the action is represented as a means to an end, and hence objectivated (see chapter 3) by means of nominalization, or by using a process noun or metonym. Again, I have already touched on this category in the previous chapter, but because of the partial overlap between legitimation and purpose some repetition is inevitable here. The essential meaning of this type of purpose construction can be glossed as "I achieve doing (or being, or having) *y* by *x*-ing," or "*x*-ing serves to achieve being (or doing, or having) *y*." The difference between the two cases lies in the presence or absence of human agency ("agentialization" versus "deagentialization"). In the first case, the purposeful action is coded as a circumstance of means with "by," "by means of," through," etc. The purposeful action becomes a method, a means to an end, but human agency is preserved:

> 7.17 The teacher remedied this by assisting him with her shoehorn.
> 7.18 Children cope with these difficulties by keeping the two worlds apart and never talking about home at school or mentioning school at home.
> 7.19 The skillful teacher can save the new entrant's face by showing herself to be on his side.

In the second case, the instrumental action is lexicalized as, for instance, "a way," "a mechanism," "a means," "a tool," etc., in relational clauses where the purposeful action becomes what Halliday (1985: 112–28) calls the carrier (in the case of an attributive clause) or the token (in case of an identifying clause). In this way, human agency disappears from view and the purposeful action itself, the "method," the "procedure," is constructed as achieving the purpose:

7.20  Formal group time is a powerful mechanism for social control.
7.21  The key to a smooth transition lies in avoiding the shock of anything sudden in the way of sights, sounds or experiences.
7.22  Pairing can be a very successful way of eliminating minor anxieties.

The other category of means-oriented purpose constructions is *technological*. Here, the emphasis lies on describing purposes as somehow built into the actions that achieve them. Human agency is again absent, and the purposeful actions are always nominated or referred to by means of a process noun. There are three subcategories: *use*, *function*, and *potentiality*.

*Use* is somewhat of an intermediate category between instrumental and technological action. The purposeful action is represented as using a *tool* (e.g., "registration is used to...") or as being potentially useful with respect to purpose (registration "can be used to," "is useful for," etc.)—the latter shades into what below we will call "potentiality." There is a remnant of agency, as a result of the realization by a passive clause with deleted agent. One can always ask "By whom?" "Who is the user?" At the same time, use itself—the goal as well as the means by which it is or can be achieved—has been determined by someone other than the user, and this restricts the extent of the user's agency:

7.23  Registration can also be used to encourage children to respond to their own names and learn each others'.
7.24  Drink time is used for the discussion of news.
7.25  Assembly may be used as an opportunity to celebrate birthdays, to launch appeals, to award praise and blame, and to reiterate school rules.

In the case of *function*, the purposeful actions are represented as though they have their purposes built in. This is typically realized by an identifying clause in which the purposeful action is token and the purpose is value, e.g., "Assembly [*token*] is [*identifying process*] a gathering to worship God [*value*]," or in which the purpose postmodifies the purposeful action in a nominal group (as in "a gathering to worship God"). In my data, this is often (but not exclusively) used to construct the purposes of objects rather than the purposes of actions. But even when it constructs the purpose of an action, that action is, in a sense, constructed as an object by the very use of this construction:

7.26  This is so you won't forget where you are.
7.27  This is to carry all your bits and pieces to school.
7.28  Assembly is a gathering of all or part of the school to worship God.
7.29  She shows her a peg on which to hang her coat.

Rather than as uniquely designed for a given purpose, the purpose of an action may also be constructed in terms of its *potential* for serving certain purposes, as realized by "facilitating" processes, such as "allow," "promote," "help," "teach," "facilitate," "build," etc., with the purposeful action as subject and the purpose as object or complement. There is again maximum objectivation of the purposeful action and irretrievable removal of human agency from it:

> 7.30  This after-school conversation trains your child to memorize a sequence of events.
>
> 7.31  This promotes healthy feet and strong arch muscles.
>
> 7.32  It helps her to develop her sense of time.

## (3)  Effective Action

Finally, purpose constructions may emphasize the outcome of actions. This was, again, already touched on in chapter 6 where I said that in such constructions "purposefulness is looked at from the other end, as it were, as something that turned out to exist in hindsight, rather than as something that could have been fully planned. As a result, the people who perform effective actions are represented as not fully able to be purposeful, not fully in control. They may be able to predict the outcome, but they cannot fully bring it about through their own actions. This requires that there is no identity between the agent of the action whose purpose is to be constructed and the agent of the action which constitutes the purpose". So instead of a goal, as in 7.33, or a means, as in 7.34, the purpose is here the *outcome* of an action, as in 7.35 (7.34 and 7.35 are made-up examples):

> 7.33  Mothers take their tots to the clinic to check their health.
>
> 7.34  Mothers check their babies' health by taking them to the clinic.
>
> 7.35  Mothers take their babies to the clinic, so the doctors can check their health.

In the case of the *result* (e.g., 7.36), the purposeful action enables or causes the actions of other persons. This is typically realized by result clauses with "so that," "that way," etc.:

> 7.36  We'll get there nice and early, so you can find your way about a bit before school starts.
>
> 7.37  Your child has to control aggressiveness, so others accept him.
>
> 7.38  Left-handed children should sit facing slightly to the right, so that the left arm is properly supported from elbow to wrist.

In the case of the *effect*, the purposeful action is itself agent or initiator of the purpose action:

> 7.39  Sending children away from home at an early age builds character.
>
> 7.40  Establishing the same routine going to and from school will make your child feel secure.
>
> 7.41  Recognizing the symptoms makes them easier to live with.

The distinctions that have been discussed are summarized in table 7.1.

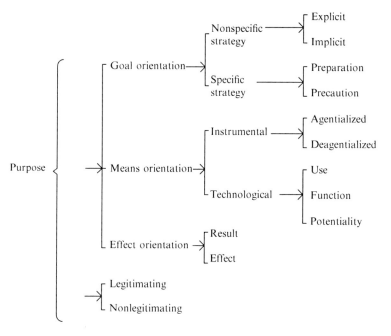

TABLE 7.1. Purpose Network

## 4. Purpose and Power: The Grammar of Purpose as a Tool for Critical Discourse Analysis

In this section, I will present an analysis of four of the texts from my "first day at school" corpus to demonstrate how the categories introduced in this chapter can be used in critical discourse analysis. The first two are the children's stories we have already discussed, *Mary Kate and the School Bus* and *Mark and Mandy*. The whole of these texts were analyzed, not just the "walking to school" episodes reproduced in examples 7.42 and 7.43:

7.42  As soon as Daddy had gone, Mummy and Mary Kate went upstairs to get dressed. Mary Kate fastened her shoes herself, just to show Mummy that she could. When she was dressed, she looked very smart—except for her hair, which was all night-wild and anyhow.

Mummy brushed out the tangles and tied the hair back with a ribbon.

"There!" said Mummy. "You'll do."

Mary Kate looked at herself in the mirror and thought she didn't look like Mary Kate at all. It was very odd. She didn't even feel like Mary Kate this morning.

"Are we going on the school bus?" she asked, as Mummy helped her into her coat.

"Not this morning," Mummy said. "We'll walk across the field. We've plenty of time. We'll get there nice and early, so you can find your way about a bit before school starts."

So they went out the back way. Mummy had to push Jacky back into the kitchen and shut the door quickly, because he wanted to go with them. They could hear him barking as they went down the garden and through the gate into the wood.

7.43 The great day came at last. Mark and Mandy were off to school for the first time. They were both very excited, and, to tell the truth, just a little nervous. Would it be easy? What would it be like? Would the teacher be strict?

Mandy was wearing a new red dress and white blouse, and felt very smart as she stood for Mummy to tie a red bow in her hair. Mark wore a green shirt and dark trousers.

Far too early for they were both so excited they could not wait, they started out, Aunt Barbara pushing Debbie in her pram, and Aunt Margaret holding on to Mandy's and Mark's hands. Smudge followed to the door.

"You'll have to wait until we get back," said Mark, and Smudge looked very sad. Where could they be going, and why were they carrying their satchels?

The two books differ considerably in the way they construct the purpose of the actions of the children, teachers, and parents. Mary Kate, an only child from a middle-class home, is constantly represented as engaged in intentional goal-oriented action:

7.44 She rubbed it with her handkerchief so as not to leave a mark on the shiny brown leather.

7.45 Mary Kate fastened her shoes herself, just to show Mummy that she could.

7.46 She stretched the elastic front of one of them to see it spring back into shape.

The same applies to her parents, and to the way they represent their own and Mary Kate's actions in the story:

7.47 Mummy slipped the pinny over Mary Kate's head to see if it fitted her.

7.48 Mummy had put all Mary Kate's things on the little blue dressing-table, ready for the morning.

7.49 "So you are," cried Daddy. "Well you better come and eat a hearty breakfast. You'll need to keep your strength up."

I analyzed two chapters from each book (amounting to approximately 3,500 words in the case of *Mary Kate* and 1,600 words in the case of *Mark and Mandy*). In *Mark and Mandy*, I found only one instance of intentional action (on the part of the parents), in *Mary Kate* there are twenty-four—and only two of these contain moralized actions (example 7.48 is one of them). The actions of Mark and Mandy, on the other hand, are not constructed as purposeful, but as the effect of physical states and emotions (7.50–7.52). Mark and Mandy's parents and teachers, similarly, do not construct as purposeful what they ask Mark and Mandy to do: in *Mark and Mandy*, things are fated (7.53) or authoritatively imposed (7.54–7.55):

7.50 Mark was so excited he could not wait.

7.51 Mandy was too happy swinging to and fro to stop.

7.52 "Oooh I am tired," she said and sat down.
7.53 Soon autumn would be here and Mark and Mandy would have to start school.
7.54 "No talking," said the teacher, and lessons began.
7.55 Then Mummy stood up, "Come along, we'll feed the ducks now."

The other two texts that I analyzed are *Your Child and Success at School* (Luck, 1990), a heavily illustrated, magazine-format booklet for parents, distributed through news agents, hence widely available, and *And So to School* (Cleave et al., 1982), an NFER-Nelson report on a study of the transition from home to school, containing many recommendations for teachers and distributed only to specialist outlets, hence not easily available to the general public. Examples 7.56 and 7.57 show how these two books represent the same "setting off for school in the morning" episode:

7.56 Start the day with a nourishing breakfast eaten in a well-protected uniform, because in the excitement your child may spill things. The family can talk calmly and happily to her about the day ahead. When she is ready with her school-bag complete with lunch box, pencil case, tissues and treasures, set off for school together with plenty of time to spare.
7.57 "Today I am going to school." Jane is up early, eager to put on her grey pinafore dress and red jumper. These are all clothes suggested by her head teacher and purchased from a local chain store. Many infant schools now adopt this practice. Her mother makes sure she has a substantial breakfast today, and instead of a leisurely look at the paper gets herself ready to take Jane to school.

I analyzed the sections from *Your Child and Success at School* which deal specifically with "the first day." They contain a total of about 1,700 words. There were only three purpose constructions which represented parents as engaged in goal-oriented action:

7.58 Display your child's school creations to show how much you appreciate them.
7.59 You should start early to avoid unnecessary stress.
7.60 You need to plan practically to ensure this milestone in your child's life passes smoothly and enjoyably.

Children's actions were constructed as goal-oriented only once ("Right-handed children will face slightly to the left, to support the right arm") and the actions of teachers only twice.

More frequent were means-oriented (seven cases, e.g., 7.61–7.63) and, especially, effect-oriented purpose constructions (eleven cases, e.g., 7.64–7.66):

7.61 Early school activities are teaching basic mathematical skills such as measurement.
7.62 It helps your child to develop her sense of time.
7.63 Establishing the same routine to and from school will make your child feel secure.
7.64 It is important for you to meet the teacher, so you have some idea of the person your child will be spending time with.

    7.65  This teacher welcomes our help with the reading lessons, so that the children can have turns of individual attention.

    7.66  Your child has to learn to control aggressiveness, so that others accept him.

Such effect-oriented constructions of parents' actions are also very common in articles about "the first day" in the family pages of tabloid and local newspapers. The writers seem to assume that parents are, in principle, not convinced of the benefits of schooling. These benefits cannot be intended by them, but only appear as the effect of actions imposed on them by expert advice and reluctantly undertaken. For the same reason, the purposes of parental action are almost always "moralized." Looked at from the point of view of the parent (and, in these texts, this is almost exclusively the mother), the handing over of their children to the education system is a sacrifice to be made for the greater good of society. No wonder that legitimation plays such a key role here and that so much emphasis is placed on "smoothness," on trying to avoid distress on the part of both mothers and children.

    The "first day" chapter from *And So to School* contains approximately 6,500 words. There are thirty goal-oriented purpose constructions, thirty-five means-oriented purpose constructions, and only two effect-oriented constructions. Children are often constructed as purposeful actors, but while the purposes of Mary Kate's actions (cleaning her shoes, trying on her clothes to see if they fit, etc.) are constructed as rational, those of the children in *And So to School* are often "irrational" or inappropriate (7.67 and 7.68), and if they are not, they are clearly moralized (e.g., 7.69).

    7.67  Rosalie, seeing a brand-new slide, eagerly ran to try it out.

    7.68  In order to get it [encouragement and approval], new children ignored queues and went straight to the teacher.

    7.69  The children use specific apparatus and movements to promote muscular coordination.

The actions of the teachers are either goal-oriented (e.g., 7.70 and 7.71) or, more frequently, means-oriented (7.72–7.74):

    7.70  The reception teachers went into the nursery unit to see their prospective pupils.

    7.71  From time to time Jane's teacher paused to explain personally to her what was going to happen next.

    7.72  "Register time" often forms part of a conscious attempt to train children in listening and responding.

    7.73  The teacher resolved this by explaining that the other children would be undressing too.

    7.74  The embarrassment which can be incurred by an individual in group situations is a potent weapon in the hands of a teacher who wants to shame a child in front of peers.

As can be seen, the purposes of the teacher's own activities are rarely moralized. They are constructed as practical solutions for the problem of "ensuring a smooth transition" and keeping order, and they are frequently means oriented. Teachers are represented as the users of methods and techniques designed by experts, and it is these means, rather than the teachers, which achieve the purpose.

As we have analyzed only a few texts, no hard and fast conclusions can be drawn. Nevertheless, some patterns emerge. First, there is a class dimension in all of this, a set of differences that relate to the social distribution of these texts. Children are endowed with purposefulness in a text which represents the middle-class home and the middle-class school—and which reaches the middle-class child. In the mass market, on the other hand, children are represented as either acting on impulse or in response to authoritative commands.

But even in the middle-class school, as represented in our examples, the child's purposefulness can become problematic. Not all of the child's own goals are appropriate. Children must learn to act according to the goals of the system. Hence, moralized purposes occur often. In the mass-marketed publication, on the other hand, neither children nor adults are represented as engaged in purposeful action. If parental behavior has the desired outcome, this is the result of following expert advice, not of implementing goals which they have set themselves.

Clearly, the discursive distribution of purposefulness has everything to do with the distribution of power in concrete social practices (here, the relations among children, parents, and teachers in the context of schooling and also the relation between educational experts and teachers) and in society generally (the class relations involved): "discourse is a place where relations of power are exercised and enacted" (Fairclough, 1989a: 43).

# The Visual Representation of
# Social Actors

In this chapter, I adapt the framework for analyzing social actors I presented in chapter 2 to the domain of visual communication and apply it to the visual representation of "others" in a variety of Western media.

## 1. Word and Image

In many contexts of communication, the division of labor between word and image is more or less as follows: words provide the facts, the explanations, the things that "need to be said in so many words"; images provide interpretations, ideologically colored angles, and they do so not explicitly, but by suggestion, by connotation, by appealing to barely conscious, half-forgotten knowledge (Berger, 1972).

Semiotic divisions of labor are historically and contextually specific. In some contexts, for instance in many domains of science and technology, visualizations are seen as the most complete and explicit way of explaining things, and words become supplements, comments, footnotes, labels. Elsewhere, visualization remains pervasive. In advertisements, the images give us the dreams of glamour or fulfillment, or the allusions to forbidden pleasures and gratifications; the words give us the information we need (if any), the specifications of the product, the addresses where we might buy it, the price. In newspapers, the words tell us what the politicians did, the images, capturing a fleeting moment, show them, for instance, as either vigorous and in control, or slumped back, seemingly defeated (Hall, 1982).

All of this was described well by Roland Barthes in *Mythologies* (1973) and in his essays on photography from the 1960s (1977). On the one hand, he said, photographic images simply mechanically reproduce what was actually there in front of the lens, and hence are as multiply interpretable as reality itself, in need of words to "fix" their meaning. On the other hand, many of the objects reproduced in this way carry associations with "where they come from," and so convey all of the values and ideas which the popular culture associates with that "place" of origin. The mode of reading that this encourages is therefore kept very open and fluid. The meanings seemingly emanate from the depicted objects themselves rather than from an act of signification. They are seemingly read into the images by the viewer, rather than being encoded into the image by the producer. Barthes described this in the celebrated *Paris Match* example (1973: 116):

> I am at the barber's and a copy of Paris-Match is offered me. On the cover, a young Negro in a French uniform is saluting, with his eyes uplifted, probably fixed on a fold of the tricolour. All this is the meaning of the picture. But, whether naively or not, I see very well what it signifies to me: that France is a great Empire, that all her sons, without any colour discrimination, faithfully serve her flag.

If this reflects how contemporary popular culture ("naively or not") construes the differences between images and words, then it means, for instance, that visually communicated racism can be much more easily denied, much more easily dismissed as "in the eye of the beholder" than verbal racism. Nederveen Pieterse (1992: 206) recounted the story of a brand of toothpaste called Darkie: before World War II, there were many brands of toothpaste which used shining white teeth in a black face on their labels and in their advertisements. When Darkie (originally produced in Hong Kong) was acquired by Colgate, American antiracist groups protested, and the name was changed to Darlie. But the stereotypical picture of a minstrel–style black face with exaggeratedly white teeth was apparently not considered racist and remained.

Many comic strips, children's books, television commercials, and entertainment programs continue to show stereotyped and demeaning images of blacks. In May 1998, a picture of a golly, a traditional "black minstrel" doll which, a generation or two ago, was as ubiquitous as the teddy bear in England, was printed on the cover of the television guide of the *Guardian*, a newspaper supposedly on the left of the political spectrum, to signal an article announcing a television program which, so the article said, poked fun at the American "fashion" of "political correctness" and reassured viewers that gollies and black minstrel shows are just good, old-fashioned, innocent fun.

It is for this reason that my examples in this chapter focus on visual racism. The consideration of images should have pride of place in any inquiry into racist discourse. If images seem to just show "what is," we need to show that they may not always be quite so. If images seem to just allude to things and never "say them explicitly," we need to make these allusions explicit.

## 2. The Image and the Viewer

In looking at how images depict people, I ask two questions: "How are people depicted?" and "How are the depicted people related to the viewer?" For convenience,

I will start with the latter. My account here is based on joint work with Gunther Kress (2007: 114–54). Three dimensions are considered: the social distance between depicted people and the viewer, the social relation between depicted people and the viewer, and the social interaction between depicted people and the viewer. In all three cases, the relation is, of course, symbolic, imaginary: we are made to see the people depicted as though they are strangers or friends, as though they are "below" us or "above" us, as though they are in interaction with us or not, and so on, whatever the actual relations between us and those people, or those kinds of people.

(1) Social Distance

In pictures, as in real life, distance communicates interpersonal relationships. We "keep our distance" from strangers (if given the chance); we are "close to" our nearest and dearest; we "work closely" with someone; and so on. Distance indicates the closeness, literally and figuratively, of our relationships, whether such closeness is temporary, lasting the duration of a particular interaction, or more permanent, and whatever more precise meaning it gains in specific contexts.

In pictures, distance becomes symbolic. People shown in a "long shot," from far away, are shown as if they are strangers; people shown in a "close-up" are shown as if they are "one of us." This is exploited in figure 8.1, which comes from a Dutch junior high school geography textbook (Bols et al., 1986). The chapter from which it is taken is titled "The Third World in Our Street." Juxtaposed are three women with head scarves and a young couple, the girl white, the boy black. The women, shown as culturally "different" (the emblematic head scarves), sticking to each other, etc., are distant, shown as "strangers," and the young couple, the instance of immigrants mixing, of cultural and social rapprochement and assimilation, as close: they are depicted as though they might be friends of the young readers of the book, or at least as people who might frequent the same places and do the same kinds of things. Never mind that some of the students for whom this book is produced might have mothers or sisters who look like the women on the left. They will now learn that, in the context of the Dutch education system, they are supposed to distance themselves from that "kind of people."

This kind of differential use of distance is common in school books dealing with questions of immigration, developing countries, and so on. In an Australian school book, with the telling title *Our Society and Others* (Oakley, 1985), Kress and I found, in a chapter on Aboriginal people, that all of the Aboriginal people in the chapter were depicted from considerable distance—from such a distance, in fact, that it was often difficult to perceive their individual characteristics. Only the overall impression came across. One woman, however, was depicted in close shot: the Aboriginal poet Kath Walker, and some lines of hers concluded the chapter (quoted in Oakley, 1985: 164):

> Dark and white upon common ground
> In club and office and social round
> Yours the feel of a friendly land
> The grip of the hand.

FIGURE 8.1. "The Third World in Our Street" (Bols et al., 1986).

(2) Social Relation

A second variable is the angle from which we see the person, and this includes the vertical angle, that is, whether we see the person from above, at eye level, or from below, and the horizontal angle, that is, whether we see a person frontally or from the side, or perhaps from somewhere in between. These angles express two aspects of the represented social relation between the viewer and the people in the picture: power and involvement.

Gunther Kress and I interpret the vertical angle as, in one way or another, related to power differences. To look down on someone is to exert imaginary symbolic power over that person, to occupy, with regard to that person, the kind of "high" position which, in real life, would be created by stages, pulpits, balconies, and other devices for literally elevating people in order to show their social elevation. To look up at someone signifies that the someone has symbolic power over the viewer, whether as an authority, a role model, or something else. To look at someone from eye level signals equality.

The horizontal angle realizes symbolic involvement or detachment. Its real-life equivalent is the difference between coming "face to face" with people, literally and figuratively "confronting" them, and occupying a "sideline" position. From such a position, we may be doing the same thing, e.g., listening to a lecture, but we don't actually communicate with each other. Just what this means precisely will, of course, be colored by the specific context. What in one context may be "ignoring each other" (e.g., sitting next to a stranger in a train) may, in another, be "experiencing something together" (e.g., listening to a concert with a loved one).

Figure 8.2 shows Burmese refugees in Bangladesh. The picture gains its power not just from what it depicts but also from how it relates the viewer (that is, us) to what it depicts. The Burmese are shown from some distance, and as viewers we are looking down on them. They are depicted as socially "below us," as low in power compared to us. Yet one of the young refugees is looking at us, from the center of the picture, and that means we are not just looking at *them*. They are also looking at *us*—a look that can, of course, be interpreted in different ways: as an appeal, or as a reproach, or both.

FIGURE 8.2. Burmese refugees in Bangladesh (John Vink, 1992). Reproduced by permission of Magnum Photos.

(3) Social Interaction

Figure 8.2 therefore also exemplifies the dimension of social interaction. Here, the crucial factor is whether or not depicted people look at the viewer. If they do not look at us, they are, as it were, offered to our gaze as a spectacle for our dispassionate scrutiny. The picture makes us look at them as we would look at people who are not aware we are looking

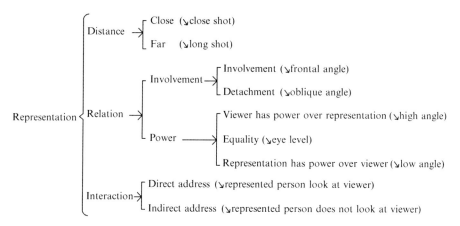

TABLE 8.1. Representation and Viewer Network

at them, as "voyeurs," rather than interactants. If they do look at us, if they do address us directly with their look, the picture articulates a kind of visual "you," a symbolic demand. The people in the picture want something from us—and what that something is, is then signified by other elements of the picture: by facial expressions, by gestures, and also by angles, e.g., by whether they look down at us or not, and whether their bodies are angled toward us or not. But exactly what do the Burmese refugees demand from us? That, the photographer does not say. That, we have to work out for ourselves.

There are three key factors, then—distance, angle, and the gaze. They are diagrammed in the system network in table 8.1. All three must always be there. One cannot portray someone in a two-dimensional picture without making choices in all three of these respects. The portrait must either be close up or far away, either from above or below or at eye level, either frontally or sideways, either looking at the viewer or not. However, the gradations and multiple combinations these dimensions allow can realize many different ways of depicting people as "others." The same image parameters can be used to show the exclusion, the keeping-at-a-distance of people, in order to accuse and critique, or to ourselves exclude and keep at a distance members of our own school class, our own community, our own country, etc., as in the case of the school textbooks.

At least three possible strategies for visually representing people as "others," as "not like us," follow from this: the strategy of *distanciation*, representing people as "not close to us," as "strangers"; the strategy of *disempowerment*, representing people as "below us," as "downtrodden" (or whatever adjective best fits the given context); and the strategy of *objectivation*, representing people as objects for our scrutiny, rather than as subjects addressing the viewer with their gaze and symbolically engaging with the viewer in this way.

## 3. Depicting People

I now move to my other question. How are people depicted? This is not an alternative to the first approach; the two dimensions are always co-present, realizing both "How are the people in the picture represented?" and "How is the viewer's relation to the people in the picture represented?"

In chapter 2, I investigated this question in relation to verbal discourse. Here, I ask the same sort of questions about pictorial references to people, in whatever medium. What options, what choices does the "language of images" give us to depict people?

## (1) Exclusion

First of all, there is always the possibility of exclusion, the possibility of not including specific people or kinds of people in representations of the groups (institutions, societies, nations, etc.) in which they live and work, and to which they therefore belong. This is always a symbolic form of social exclusion, not acknowledging the existence of certain people or kinds of people who live and work among us. In a much-publicized case, an American car advertisement showing Ford workers was used in Europe—without the black workers. They had been removed by means of Photoshop image manipulation techniques. This is a racist exclusion. It can only be assumed to stem from the idea that Europeans will assign negative characteristics to those black workers, and hence to Ford. During the Gulf War, I collected all of the Gulf War photographs from two Australian newspapers (I was living in Australia at the time). There were many shots of individual soldiers from the Allied forces, often imbued with a touch of heroism. They did not include any black soldiers.

To take a very different kind of example, as we will see in chapter 9, Playmobil toys present children with a vast range of different social types. There are ambulance drivers, police officers, doctors, patients, teachers, schoolchildren, families in large Victorian mansions, and families in small suburban houses—but there are no black, brown, or yellow people. Playmobil does, however, sell a box called "ethnic family." This family is different from "non-ethnic" families in several ways: they look more like each other, there are more children (three instead of two), there is more difference between the generations, and they do not come with a set of accessories to allow them to do things or to be put in specific settings. They are offered as decontextualized specimens.

## (2) Roles

The people in pictures may be depicted as involved in some action or not, and, if they are involved in an action, they may be the "agents," the doers of that action, or the "patients," the people to whom the action is done. An important aspect here is, of course, what they do or what is done to them—and which of the things they may in reality do or have done to them are not shown.

Nederveen Pieterse's book *White on Black: Images of Africa and Blacks in Western Popular Culture* (Nederveen Pieterse, 1992) is based on images collected for an exhibition of European "negrophilia" and contains 262 illustrations from that collection, originally taken from books, cartoons, comic strips, product labels, and so on. In these illustrations, blacks are almost always shown as agents doing things to or for white people—with two common exceptions, both occurring only in representations dating from the colonial era. The first is being washed. There was a common joke of trying to wash a black child and not getting the black off, a "hopeless task," as one Dutch postcard showing this scene was captioned. A children's book popular in my childhood had a rhyme beginning *moriaantje, zo zwart as roet* (*moriaantje*, black as soot); the word *moriaantje* is actually not a name but a category: "little Moor," "little black." The second is being baptized: this was common in the many pictures of missionary activities which used to circulate, and perhaps still do in certain circles.

The things black people are shown as doing include (in no particular order): begging (for instance, in hunger campaigns), cannibalism, dancing and playing music (usually in exaggerated, contorted poses), serving drinks to white people, holding mirrors up for white people, (men) consorting with white women, eating bananas, carrying heavy loads, bowing, running, making black power salutes, and casting magic spells. In other words, blacks are depicted in low, subservient jobs and in activities which are either represented as "wild" and "uncivilized" or as downright evil. Things done by whites to blacks were not represented here.

Depicting people in roles of this kind symbolically oppresses them, symbolically excludes them from certain roles and confines them to others. It also clearly associates them with subservient or negative roles and actions. This does not have to be racist. It could also relate to cultural rather than racial prejudices. Peasants, workers, women, children, and all kinds of other groups have been treated in this way. But as soon as racially categorized people are shown in roles of this kind, it becomes racist and realizes the specific themes of racist discourse, as is clear from the activities included in the "negrophilia" collection.

## (3) Specific and Generic

There is also the question of whether people are depicted specifically or generically. In the case of language, this distinction is of evident importance for the study of racist discourse. Are we talking about a specific Jewish or black person, or about Jews and blacks in general? Moving from the one to the other is, in this context, almost always moving from specific judgments to prejudice and racism. At first sight, it might seem that images can only show specific people. Yet, there is a difference between concentrating the depiction on what makes a person unique and concentrating the depiction on what makes a person into a certain social type. When people are photographed as desirable models of current styles of beauty and attractiveness, their individuality can seem to disappear behind what categorizes them—behind the hairdo, the makeup, the dress, the status accessories. And what categorizes people need not, of course, only be dress and hairstyle and grooming, it may also be stereotyped facial characteristics. Cartoons and comic strips often present such stereotyped depictions.

As Nederveen Pieterse points out (1992: 26–29), in paintings by Rembrandt, Rubens, and others, blacks were still depicted as specific individuals, and there was not yet a trace of the schematic black physiognomies which would develop later. In contrast to language, however, the distinction between specific and generic is not a hard and fast either-or distinction in pictures. The specific and generic often mix, with all of the possibilities of "naturalizing" the stereotype which this offers.

FIGURE 8.3. *Punch* cartoon.

(4)  Individuals and Groups

People may be depicted as individuals or groups. In my collection of photographs from the first Gulf War, Allied soldiers are usually depicted as individuals and Iraqi soldiers as groups. The members of such groups can then be all similar to each other to different degrees, in other words, the "they're all the same," "you can't tell them apart" principle can be applied to different degrees. In the Gulf War photographs, it was often the posing of the soldiers which homogenized them and diminished individual differences. In figure 8.3, a *Punch* cartoon from the 1920s, homogenization is taken to the extreme: all of the black band members look exactly the same.

(5)  Categorization

In chapter 2, I discussed the ways in which people can be linguistically categorized. Visual categorization is primarily a matter of whether people are categorized in terms of "cultural" or "biological" characteristics, or in terms of some combinations of these. Cultural categorization is signified by means of standard attributes, attributes commonly used to categorize these groups: items of dress or hairdo, for instance, such as the head scarves and hijabs in figure 8.4. Such attributes need not be caricatured or exaggerated, their presence is enough. They work through connotation; they connote the negative or positive values and associations attached to a particular sociocultural group by the sociocultural group for which the representation is in the

FIGURE 8.4. Muslim women. Reproduced by permission of Magnum Photos.

FIGURE 8.5. Muslim women (Elke Boch, 2001).

first place produced. The choice of this method of representation indicates that these characteristics are considered to be cultural, hence in principle changeable by the group whose characteristics they are.

The photographs reproduced in figures 8.4 and 8.5 were used in an article in the *Guardian Weekend* which appeared a few months after the attacks of 9/11 (8 December 2001) under the title "The Other Side of the Veil." Although the women in figure 8.4 are relatively close to the viewer, they are "looked down upon," like the Burmese refugees in figure 8.2. They also form a large group which is strongly homogenized through the very similar poses and through the focus on the head coverings. And although they wear a variety of hijabs and veils (which would have a variety of class and other meanings to the initiated), to Western eyes their head coverings may look very similar and create a "they are all the same" effect—all the same, that is, with the exception of the one woman who does not wear any form of head covering, whose eyes form the central point of focus of the picture. The women in figure 8.5, on the other hand, are individualized and represented as specific people rather than types by being separately framed and by the backgrounding of the head coverings which three of them are wearing. They also look directly at the viewer, in closely framed eye-level shots. They are depicted as close to us, the viewers, regardless of whether they wear head coverings or not. In short, this article juxtaposes two different ways of looking at Muslim women—one in which they are represented as equals and brought close to "us," *Guardian* readers, and one in which they are homogenized and looked down upon, with the exception of the one woman who is depicted as not "like them." This is in keeping with the article's introduction, which asks, "So is Islam all about female oppression? Or can it offer a kind of freedom?" (*Guardian Weekend*, 8 December 2001: 15).

Biological categorization uses standardized exaggerations of physical features to connote the negative or positive associations which the represented sociocultural group evokes for the sociocultural group for which the representation is primarily produced. The choice of this method of representation indicates that the characteristics are considered to be "biological," "in the blood," and hence ineradicable. The unrealistic exaggeration of physical features indicates that they are not just meant to enable recognition, but also have symbolic value, a symbolic value which is essentially cultural and whose relation with physical features must be discursively constructed and disseminated before it can be perceived. This, in turn, means that biological characterization can only be fully understood if an element of historical iconography is introduced into the investigation.

The stereotyped black person, for instance, has exaggeratedly white teeth and eyes. In the United States, this signifier developed out of comparisons with raccoons (hence the derogatory slang word "coons" for "blacks"), animals of the night with a reputation of being sly thieves (Nederveen Pieterse, 1996: 135). Initially, the comparison was still explicit, still visible; later, it became naturalized as a stereotyped part of black physiognomy. The typical "minstrel" image is partly based on it.

Exaggeratedly protruding lower parts of faces and thick lips were invested with meaning by nineteenth-century racist anthropologists; this meaning had not yet been invented when painters like Rogier van der Weyden, Rembrandt, Rubens, and so on painted blacks. Racist scientists like Georges Cuvier explicitly related physiognomical signifiers to negative cultural characteristics and explicitly construed these as innate and ineradicable:

> The negro race is confined to the south of Mount Atlas. It is marked by a black complexion, crisped or woolly hair, compressed cranium, and flat nose. The projection of the lower parts of the face and the thick lips evidently approximate it to the monkey tribe. The hordes of which it consists have always remained in the most complete state of utter barbarism. (quoted in Nederveen Pieterse, 1996: 143)

As Freud has shown, and as is demonstrated by any clown's act, exaggeration is also humorous. What is now taboo as serious science and no longer explicitly formulated lives on as humor in children's books, comic strips, television commercials, etc. For the critics of racism, it may be more important to attend to the visual racism in apparently "humorous," "innocent," and "entertainment" contexts than to more blatant forms of racism, including the few scientists, crackpot newspaper commentators, and public figures who still produce explicitly racist theories and diatribes.

Table 8.2 summarizes the types of categorization I have discussed in this section.

At least five different strategies for visually representing people as "others" follow from the discussion in this section:

- the strategy of exclusion, not representing people at all in contexts where, in reality, they are present
- the strategy of depicting people as the agents of actions which are held in low esteem or regarded as subservient, deviant, criminal, or evil
- the strategy of showing people as homogeneous groups and thereby denying them individual characteristics and differences ("they're all the same")
- the strategy of negative cultural connotations
- the strategy of negative racial stereotyping

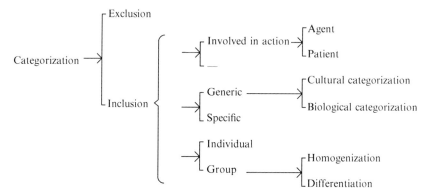

TABLE 8.2. Visual Social Actor Network

These strategies can occur in many different combinations and often admit of degrees. By themselves, many of them need not necessarily be tied to cultural prejudice or racism in the narrowest senses of the terms, that is, as I take them here, as something historically specific, something directly related to particular histories of oppression, in the case of racism, and class differences, which have restricted opportunities in the context of the European and North American colonization of non-European peoples, and the whole aftermath of that history. But combined with negative (or indeed positive) racial stereotyping, all other strategies become racist and add significant themes and dimensions to racist discourse. And similarly, combined with negative (and positive) cultural connotations, all other strategies also become strategies of cultural prejudice, for instance, of ethnic prejudice, and add significant dimensions and themes to culturally prejudiced discourses.

Let me conclude by returning to figure 8.1, to show how the strategies I have outlined in this chapter come together in a specific instance. First, in the picture on the left, the women (1) are culturally categorized, generic, and shown as a relatively homogeneous group; (2) connote something like "Middle East"/"Islam"; and (3) are distanced from us, literally shown as being "on the other side of the street," yet in a Dutch environment (the bicycles). The picture on the right contrasts with this in that the boy and the girl are (1) categorized by means of their blonde hair and black skin, but also to a much greater degree represented as specific individuals, and (2) much closer to us, the viewers. When these elements are put together, grasped visually, in a single glance, a message is conveyed which goes, perhaps, something like this:

> Distance yourself from cultural "others," especially if they are "Islamic" and from older generations of immigrants who do not assimilate to the country they're in and stay on their own side of the street. Attach yourself and become close to the new generation, where youth cultures mix, absorb different cultural elements, and engage in common activities: the color of your skin and hair will no longer matter so long as that kind of coming together is possible.

# Representing Social Actors with Toys

In this chapter, I investigate children's toys as a semiotic resource for representing social roles and identities in play, focusing specifically on the Playmobil range of toys and drawing on the social actor theory I introduced in chapter 2.

## 1. Introduction

In chapter 2, I introduced a framework for analyzing the linguistic resources of English for constructing representations of the roles and identities of social actors, and in chapter 8, I presented a similar framework for the visual representation of social actors. Here, I continue this line of inquiry by looking at toys (more specifically, dolls and figurines) as a semiotic resource for representing social roles and identities in play. Playmobil offers children many different social types, together with accessories that associate them with particular activities. How does it structure the social world for them? Which roles and identities are included? Which excluded? As we will see, toys, too, can be seen as discourse. Playmobil offers quite specific perspectives on race and gender, for instance.

I will begin with an overview of the kinds of roles, identities, and meanings that dolls and figurines can convey, based, for the most part, on the three main categories of dolls included in the Toys as Communication research program: display dolls such as Barbies, Sindies, and action men (see Caldas-Coulthard and Van Leeuwen, 2002), teddy bears (see Caldas-Coulthard and Van Leeuwen, 2003), and Playmobil figures. The toys used as examples were collected in 1998 and 1999. The second part of the chapter deals more specifically with preschool Playmobil, analyzing the full range of 20 boxes with their 40 characters and 102 accessories.

Elsewhere (Van Leeuwen, 2005a: 3), I have argued that social semioticians engage in three kinds of activities:

1. collecting, documenting, and systematically cataloging semiotic resources (including their history)
2. investigating how these resources are used in specific historical, cultural, and institutional contexts and how people talk about them in these contexts: plan them, teach them, justify them, critique them, etc.
3. contributing to the discovery and development of new semiotic resources and new ways of using existing semiotic resources

This chapter focuses for the most part on the structure of Playmobil as a semiotic resource, on what is and what is not included in Playmobil, and on the way Playmobil characters and accessories are designed and marketed to communicate a particular perspective on the social world. In addition, toys are designed for play, and playing can be seen as a (very visible) way of "reading" that message according to the needs and interests of the situation and of the individual child. For this reason, we also video recorded children at play with Playmobil in two settings, preschool and home. The final section of the chapter will include some of this material to demonstrate that Playmobil is not always "read" as it was designed to be read, that what children actually do with Playmobil is by no means fully determined by its design, but also by contextual rules and by the specific needs and interests of specific, individual children within that context. This will bring out two important dimensions of social semiotics. First, the rules that connect signifiers and signifieds and the rules that connect signs together into utterances are *social* rules, rules made by people to regulate semiotic production and interpretation according to contextually specific needs and interests. Second, semiotic production and interpretation are multimodal. Although Playmobil is a distinct "system," in children's play it is often freely mixed with other toys and other toy systems (and with speech and gesture)—unless there are specific contextual rules prohibiting this, as in the preschool where we filmed, where small groups of children, seated around an "activity table," were only given one kind of Playmobil (only the pirates, or only the firemen, for instance). Yet, for all of this multimodality and contingency, children will also become aware of the specific potentials and constraints of Playmobil and, indeed, of any other semiotic system. As they are playing, they will gradually learn what can and cannot easily be done and "said" with Playmobil, the way it bends itself easily to some meanings and resists others, the difference between what children want to say and what Playmobil (or the adults who may regulate its use) wants children to say.

## 2. Roles, Identities, Meanings

This section will provide an overview of the way their design can define dolls in terms of their roles, their identities, and the meanings they may, as symbolic representations, convey over and above these roles and identities.

## (1) Roles

Dolls may or may not be designed *kinetically*, that is, they may or may not have parts that move or can be made to move by the child (Van Leeuwen and Caldas-Coulthard, 2004). Such kinetically designed dolls may either be "interactive" or "active." By "interactive," I mean here that the dolls are designed to have things done *to* them by the child. They are not in the first place designed for interacting with other dolls in representational play; they are designed to interact with the child directly, whether in role play or otherwise. Teddy bears, for instance, have a soft fur to encourage the child to cuddle and stroke them. Other dolls, too, may have specific interactive design features: clothes that can be taken off, hair that can be combed, a mouth that takes a baby's bottle. Rag dolls, too, are interactive in this way; their flexibility makes it possible to do all kinds of things to them or with them. Tamagotchi dolls are another example.

In other cases, the doll is kinetically designed for representational play, designed to allow the child to make the *doll* do specific things or assume specific poses. I will say that a doll is kinetically designed as an "actor" if its design allows the child to make that doll perform one or more autonomous actions, e.g., an action man that can throw a hand grenade, a wind-up doll that can play the drums, a baby doll that can cry, a Sindy that can swim in the bath. Such actions may be hand-driven as, e.g., in the case of glove puppets, or powered in some way, as in the case of the hand-grenade-throwing action man and the swimming Sindy, which have elastic bands in their joints that can be "wound up" by rotating their arms and/or legs. I will say that a doll is kinetically designed as a "model" if its design allows the child to make it assume a range of *poses*, through articulated or flexible limbs, as in the case of display dolls such as Barbies. Clearly, a doll can have both active and interactive features. Many teddy bears (but not all) have fairly rigid but articulated limbs (like baby dolls) and are also made of soft, cuddly material (unlike most baby dolls). The terms we introduce here index elements of design that can combine in various ways, rather than unique classifications. It should also be remembered that children can (and do) make dolls move in certain ways even when they have not been designed to do so. They can make totally rigid dolls walk, fly, swim, and so on. Yet, even when their play does not follow the scenario that has been built into the doll, children will register that what they are doing is not what the doll was made for, and in the process they will, in a very tactile way, come to understand the differences between different roles, the differences, for instance, between what Halliday (1985) calls the "initiator" in a causative construction (the "puppeteer" who *makes* others, in this case, dolls, do things) and the "actor" who does things him- or herself, or the differences between actions that affect the material world and encounter its resistances (swimming, throwing hand grenades, etc.) and "behaviors" that do not (e.g., Barbie's coy or action man's threatening poses).

## (2) Identities

Dolls only have a specific, individual identity when they are, intentionally, given unique facial features, and this is normally only the case with handmade dolls, e.g., many nineteenth-century porcelain and wax dolls, expensive "art" dolls, and home-made dolls. Most dolls are "generic," whether as a result of the standard "patterns" used to make handmade dolls or as a result of mass production. Most dolls are also nameless—generic characters, standard types, identifiable only in terms of their function or class, designed to represent categories such as "baby," "black person," "fireman," etc., as in the case of Playmobil. Children may of course give names to "nameless" dolls; the point here is, however, that a specific or named identity is not part of either the doll's design or its marketing. If dolls do come with names, they have the names of standard characters or types (Punch and Judy, Barbie and Ken) or of individual fictional characters (e.g., Paddington Bear) which have become types through mass production and distribution (so that it has become possible to speak of "a" Paddington Bear). There are also "families" of dolls, for instance, in the case of teddy bears you can have, in order of genericity, "bear," "teddy bear," "Pooh Bear." Special collectors' Barbies include many characters which are neither Barbie nor Ken, but still have the typical "Barbie" size and build, for instance, "Professor Higgins." This is not the same thing as "collectivization" (see below), as they are not necessarily designed to be played with together or sold as sets. The iconography of dolls as a medium of representing the world is clearly every bit as complex as the iconography of Renaissance art (e.g., Hermeren, 1969: ch. 2).

There are two other key identity features. The first relates to an issue I have already mentioned: individuality versus collectivity. A doll can be designed and marketed as a stand-alone, an individual, or as a "collectivity," a set, intended to be played with as such, e.g., a Playmobil family or a set of tin soldiers. Here, the identity of the doll derives from its membership in a group and is signified by shared physical and/or cultural attributes. A set may also be dyadic, including just two dolls, e.g., a couple such as Barbie and Ken. This is again realized by shared and complementary physical and/or cultural attributes, by making matching or complementary outfits available (e.g., matching beach outfits for Ken and Barbie), and by marketing them as a dyad. It signifies that their identity is to be taken as at least in part deriving from their membership in the dyad.

If we compare these elements of identity with their counterparts in language, an important difference emerges. In language, naming is not uniquely associated with the generic. It provides resources for designating things as either specific or generic and as either individual or collective. In the case of toys—at least as they are designed and marketed—the distinction between the unique individual and the mass-produced specimen is blurred, and the child must create the doll's individuality him- or herself. As a result, the question of individual identity plays a significant role in many children's stories featuring dolls and teddy bears. In a typical plot, the mass-produced toy acquires a unique identity either through wear and tear or as the result of a mistake during production. In *My Old Teddy* (Mansell, 1991), for instance, the protagonist's teddy first loses a leg, which is then repaired by her mother. Next, her brother rips off an arm, and again it is repaired. Next, an ear comes off as a result of rough play, and again it is repaired. But when finally the head comes off, the mother declares that teddy "has had enough" and gives her daughter a new teddy. But, says the daughter, "I love poor old Teddy best"; it is, of course, precisely his unique appearance, by now covered in stitches, patches, and bandages, that makes "old Teddy" so unique, individual, and lovable. "Ruby" (Glen, 1997) begins with a scene in a factory where "Mrs. Harris had been day-dreaming when she made Ruby." As a result, Ruby accidentally acquires a spotted belly and a nose which is sewn on in a crooked way. After various misadventures, Ruby ends up in a secondhand store, where she is picked out by Susie for her individuality (ibid.: 31): "That's the one," said the little girl. "Yes, Susie," said Grandfather, "that one looks very special."

Finally, I will say that the identity of a doll is "physical" if it is signified by means of physical attributes such as, typically, build, facial features, skin color, and color and type of hair or, more generally, features that cannot be changed, for in the world of dolls, items of dress can become fixed, quasi-physical attributes. I will say that the identity of a doll is "cultural" if it is signified by means of cultural attributes (typically, dress, hairdo, etc.) or, more generally, by attributes which can be changed. In the world of dolls, what is "physical" and immutable, and what is "cultural" and transformable, can be articulated in complex ways. The gender of a baby doll, for instance, may be signified as "physical" if the doll has genitals (as some do) or as "cultural" if the doll can be dressed either as a girl or a boy, but has no physical gender features.

## (3)  Meanings

So far, I have discussed dolls that are designed to represent "realistic" social roles and identities. Other dolls represent exaggerated characters or introduce an element of fantasy. The traits which make them unrealistic then provide clues to their symbolic meaning.

Sometimes, a doll *fuses* two distinct identities. The typical teddy bear, for instance, fuses an animal (because of the fur and the snout, and sometimes the short tail) and a very young child (because of the proportions of the body). This kind of fusion corresponds to Freud's category of "condensation" and, in good Freudian fashion, conveys a culturally "repressed" message about the nature of the child, based on the ambivalent feelings we may have about children as being, on the one hand, already human and, on the other hand, still "wild" and in need of being "tamed," "civilized"; on the one hand, "innocent" and, on the other hand, "dangerous" (in horror films, the "demonic" child is a recurring type). It may also be that the identity of a doll is set both in the real contemporary world and in either a temporally distant or mythical world; in the case of dolls, these two are not always easily separated, regardless of whether it concerns the idyllic world of Victorian childhood or some future world of superheroes, monsters, and aliens. This corresponds to Freud's category of "displacement." The Barbie catalog includes several examples. In each case, a thoroughly contemporary body combines with "period" or "mythical" dress (e.g., the already mentioned "Professor Higgins" Barbie, or Barbie-as-Cinderella), and so further inflects the multiple-layered "character" of Barbie.

Finally, certain features of a character may be represented as excessively small or large, whether for comic effect or for other, more "fetishistic" reasons (e.g., large breasts or muscles in characters from some computer games).

The categories introduced above are summarized in table 9.1. This network can be used as a tool for critical discourse analysis, to generate questions about how dolls

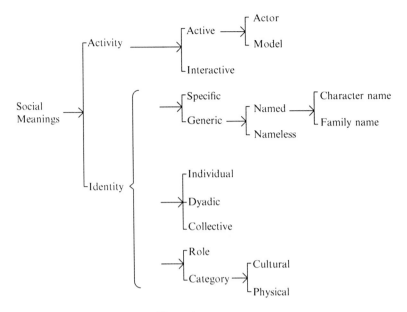

TABLE 9.1. Toy Social Actor Network

represent the social world, for instance: "When is gender treated as a 'physical' and when as a 'cultural' category?" "How often are female dolls 'actors' as opposed to 'models'?" "What individualized black dolls are there?" "What are the main themes in anthropomorphic animal or personified machines (e.g., Thomas the Tank Engine)?"

## 3. Preschool Playmobil

In this section, I will use the framework introduced above to discuss some of the key characteristics of preschool Playmobil, or 1.2.3 Playmobil, as it is called by the manufacturer.

(1) Models

Preschool Playmobil characters are primarily designed as miniature "models," that is, they are designed to allow children to "pose" them by using their articulated limbs. The options are fairly limited. The characters can either stand or sit, and they can also look at things (by turning the head). This means they are capable only of "behavioral," nontransactive action. They cannot hold objects as can Playmobil characters for older children. This is also evident from the pictures on the packaging and in the catalogs. Even if a preschool Playmobil character is shown, e.g., in the driver's seat of a car, it is not shown as actually driving the car, but as sitting in the car and looking at the viewer, as "posing" rather than as "doing" (figure 9.1). This is not the case with the packaging and the catalog pictures of Playmobil for older children.

FIGURE 9.1. "Father." Reproduced by
permission of Playmobil ® Germany.

This also means that preschool Playmobil characters are not "interactive" in
the sense that they can be "dressed" or "undressed" (e.g., by removing a helmet).
There are, of course, reasons of safety behind this. Small parts can be dangerous
for very young children. Preschool Playmobil figures are also somewhat larger than
Playmobil characters for older children. Yet, despite the rationale, the message will
be conveyed that helmets, grey hair, farmers' caps, women's long hair, and so on are
basic attributes, indelible, fixed characteristics of specific social types.

(2) Individuality

Preschool Playmobil characters may be individually or collectively identified.
This depends on the way they are packaged as individuals or groups. Here are
some of the groups: the "ethnic family"; the "family"; a mother, daughter, and
baby (in a bathroom box; catalog no. 6614); and a grandfather, grandmother, and
cat (figure 9.2).

Couples include male and female horse riders, the farmer and his wife, and the
grandparents. Clearly, family identity plays an important role in preschool Playmobil.
There are fathers, mothers, brothers, sisters, babies, grandfathers, grandmothers, and
pets (taken separately, these can become men, women, boys, girls, babies, old men,
old women). Yet some family members, here the "father" and the "grandparents," are
also separately marketed and therefore also have identities that are separate from the
family (figure 9.3). In other words, family identity is relational, deriving from your
relations with others, and also some members, most notably the father (figure 9.1)
and the grandparents, also have identities that are separate from that.

FIGURE 9.2. "Grandparents."
Reproduced by permission of
Playmobil ® Germany.

FIGURE 9.3. "Family." Reproduced by permission of Playmobil ®
Germany.

(3) Social Types

Preschool Playmobil characters are also nameless and generic, social *types*,
even in their identities as fathers, mothers, brothers, sisters, and so on, and they
represent the social world with a certain conceptual realism (Kress and Van
Leeuwen, 2006). There are, in preschool Playmobil, no characters drawn from
fiction, no anthropomorphic animals or aliens, and the cars and houses are res-
olutely contemporary, without any fantasy, anachronistic, or futuristic features.
Playmobil for older children, however, does have fantasy characters, historical
characters, aliens, and so on, and increasingly so. It is as if a solid foundation of
close-to-home reality must be laid before the world of pirates, fairy-tale princesses,
wizards, witches, and Wild West characters can be entered. Yet the everyday world
of preschool Playmobil is conceptual. It does not realistically reproduce what is
out there in the world, as in the case, for instance, of Matchbox miniature cars.
There is, in this world, only one kind of car, the basic car (figure 9.1), a car which
has the minimum features any car must have to be able to be recognized as a car,
no more and no less.

What makes people into types in this world? Essentially four things: professional
and leisure activities, gender, race, and age. All of these elements of identity are
signified by specific simple identity-marking attributes (the road worker's truck
and danger sign, the police officer's traffic light and car, and so on)—and, in the
world of preschool Playmobil, no difference exists, as yet, between "leisure activities," such as horse riding, and professions. Another category runs across all of
this: the category of social class. There are three social classes, each with a distinct,
recognizable key attribute. Professions with high-ranking status are signified by
uniforms with caps that bear the insignias of their rank, e.g., captains or police officers
(figure 9.4).

FIGURE 9.4. "Captain."
Reproduced by permission of
Playmobil ® Germany.

High-risk professions or roles have helmets and uniforms, e.g., horse riders, firemen; and lower-ranking occupations wear overalls and caps without insignias, e.g., tow truck drivers or road workers (figure 9.5).

Some intermediate forms exist, for instance, the ambulance driver, who has no cap but also does not wear overalls. In other words, the key distinctions here are those of rank (caps with or without visors and with or without insignias) and status (with or without overalls). The identity of the road worker, therefore, is determined both by the activity in which he engages, as signified by his truck and danger sign, and by his class, as signified by his dress.

Gender is signified by a small vocabulary of variations in hairstyle. Adult women either have long hair which bobs out on the side or wear their hair in a bun. Older women and black women wear their hair in a bun; younger, white women do not. As a result, older women and black women lack a feature of "female attractiveness." Color and style of dress do not strongly differentiate between male and female, but there is a sharp distinction between male and female activities. The baby, finally, can only sit and has a "male" hairstyle.

Race is signified by the color of skin and hair: brown skin, black hair. It can be noted that in the group marketed as "the family" (figure 9.3), the different family members (mother, father, son, daughter) have different hair colors, whereas all members of the "ethnic family" (figure 9.6) have the same hair color. The individuality of

FIGURE 9.5. "Road worker."
Reproduced by permission of
Playmobil ® Germany.

FIGURE 9.6. "Ethnic family."
Reproduced by permission of
Playmobil ® Germany.

the members of this family is therefore less marked. They also have more children than the family in figure 9.3.

Old age (figure 9.2) is signified both by "physical" attributes (grey hair) and "cultural" attributes (brown and grey clothes with painted-on motifs and textures, e.g., a wool cardigan for the grandfather).

(4) Activities

Playmobil characters are packaged with accessories that suggest preferred activities. Through these accessories, they are defined, not just by their "physical" and "cultural" attributes, but also by their activities. There is only one exception to this. In the "ethnic family," neither the family nor its individual members are accompanied by any accessories, such as a house, furniture, a car, tools, etc.

The accessories of the grandparents (or old people generally) speak for themselves (rocking chair, lounge suite, cozy stove, chess table, large cupboard, clock, table, light) as do the accessories of the white family, as ordered by the layout of their house: *kitchen* with dining table, stove, dishwasher, cupboard; *bedroom* with bed, cot, sideboard, baby's dressing table; *exterior* with car, boat on trailer, trees; *bathroom* (female family members only) with bath, mirror, shower, toilet, washbasin.

Apart from being almost exclusively male, professional activities are dominated by mobility: the *father* (available as part of the family box but also, and as the only member of his family, separately, with car): car, suitcase with airplane label; the *policeman*: car, traffic light; the *ambulance man*: ambulance; the *fireman*: fire truck, danger sign; the *pilot*: plane, wind vane; the *tow truck operator*: tow truck, danger sign; the *road worker*: truck, danger sign; the *captain*: boat, fish, buoy; the *farmer*: tractor and trailer, cow, pig, bag of wheat; the *horse rider*: horses, hurdles, bushes.

The only characters whose accessories do not involve mobility are the old man (rocking chair), the shepherd (pen with sheep, dog, some trees), and the farmer and his wife as a couple (pigs, cows, feeding trough, dog, bag of wheat). Separately, however, the farmer has a tractor and trailer. Mobility is therefore signified as exclusively male, with the single exception of the female horse rider.

I hope this brief analysis of preschool Playmobil (as it was in 1999) has demonstrated that the way in which this toy system is designed and marketed provides a model of society structured by organizing principles, such as work and leisure, age, gender, ethnicity, and class, and by the difference between the private and the public world, and all of these social categories have been marked with clear, visible attributes. I will now conclude with some observations of the way this societal model is used in play.

## 4. Playing with Playmobil

As part of this study of Playmobil, video recordings were made of two- to four-year-old children playing with Playmobil in a preschool in Birmingham, England. During the filming, the researcher sat on the floor with the children, letting the play episodes develop, but occasionally intervening to ask the children to identify specific characters. This did not appear to disturb the children nor interrupt the flow of the play, and yielded additional data, as can be seen in example 9.1.

The preschool imposed specific rules on the children's play. All children were seated, in groups of six, around "activity tables." One of these activity tables was devoted to Playmobil, but only of one kind, in this case firemen (this set is in fact a set for older children, rather than part of the preschool Playmobil range). The interaction was at times quite chaotic, with several conversations and actions happening at the same time, and the children often snatched characters or accessories from each other, without being overly disturbed by this. As we start, the researcher places the firemen set on the table. It includes ladders and other firefighting implements, such as a mattress (for people trapped in a building to jump on) and a spade (to throw sand on the fire). In 9.1, I focus on Page (two and a half years old), without indicating all of the simultaneous actions and utterances of the other children.

> 9.1 Page grabs a fireman in each hand.
>
> > RESEARCHER:   Who's that?
> > PAGE:   He's a fireman!
>
> She drops one of the firemen and tries to fit a hat on the other one, but fails to do so. After a while she gives up and picks up a ladder.
>
> > PAGE:   Ladder! Ladder!
>
> She puts the ladder down and grabs the mattress, then looks around, as if searching for something quite specific among the toys on the table. The boy next to her, who has been trying to make a fireman climb a ladder, puts his ladder on Page's mattress. When he is momentarily distracted, she grabs the mattress for herself again and lays the fireman on it, using the mattress as a bed.
>
> > RESEARCHER:   Who is that?
> > PAGE:   It's a baby.
>
> The researcher points at the two firemen Page is holding in her right hand.
>
> > RESEARCHER:   And that one, who is that one?
> > PAGE:   This is Mama, look.
> > RESEARCHER:   And who is that one?
> > PAGE:   It's Daddy.

> Page looks at the toys again, grabs the spade, and starts using it as a spoon to feed the "fireman-baby" on the mattress.

Already, Page can recognize a fireman. Maybe she has been read books about firemen. Firemen are after all recurrent figures in books for very young children. But she is able to perceive other affordances as well, for instance, the size of the fireman, who is very small, especially in comparison to the mattress. He could also be a baby. So she uses the fireman, the mattress, and the spade not to enact a heroic rescue, but interactively, to act out a mother-and-baby scenario in which she plays the role of the mother.

Kieran (four years old) was given a much wider range of Playmobil toys at home. It included some preschool Playmobil characters and accessories as well as ones from sets for older children. He was filmed by his father. The researcher was sitting on the floor next to him. We had included the "ethnic family" because Kieran is black, but he did not use any of the members of the "ethnic family." As the episode starts, Kieran is trying to open a plastic bag:

> 9.2  RESEARCHER:   I'll open it for you.... There you go.
>
> She hands the contents of the bag to Kieran—a bike and a bike rider. Kieran takes it and smiles.
>
> KIERAN:   Who is riding on the bike now? Who is riding on the bike?
> RESEARCHER:   This is the biker.
>
> Kieran tries to put the biker onto the bike for a brief moment, but then throws him back on the pile of Playmobil toys and surveys the toys, his hands folded in front of his face, almost as if praying. After a while, he picks up another Playmobil character. It is a wizard with a long pointed beard.
>
> KIERAN:   This is the biker.
>
> He tries to put the wizard on the bike, but as he has not been designed to sit on a bike, he does not fit. Kieran keeps trying, increasingly frustrated, and then hands the bike and the biker to the researcher.
>
> KIERAN:   Can you help me?
>
> The researcher tries for a moment.
>
> RESEARCHER:   Perhaps it's not the biker.
>
> She puts the wizard down, picks up the actual biker, puts him on, and hands biker and bike to Kieran. Kieran looks at it for a while, then puts it down, and picks up another Playmobil figure. He is not smiling any more, and he has lost interest in the bike and the biker.
>
> KIERAN:   This is a little baby.

Clearly, Kieran wanted to create a character who does not feature in the ordered world of Playmobil. He associated the bike not with a neatly helmeted, nondescript rider, but with a 'Hell's Angel'–style biker. The straggly beard and unkempt appearance of the wizard were close enough for him. But this was something you cannot "say" in the language of Playmobil, an "ungrammatical" statement. The wizard was not designed to fit onto the motorbike. The researcher could not help him and in fact suggested the "proper" solution, but Kieran had already lost interest, giving up on the idea of a wild biker and, tellingly, turning to a little baby instead.

It would be easy to argue, on the basis of the first example, for the infinite malleability of Playmobil as a resource. Playmobil did not force Page into narrowly defined roles and interactions. It turned out to be usable not just as a resource for representational play; it could also be used interactively. It would also be easy to overstate the other case, the constraints imposed by the system, the way it does not allow "deviant" meanings. Semiotic systems are always a mixture of affordance and constraint, even already in childhood. Yet some are more flexible than others. Construction toys such as Lego in its original form offered few constraints and allowed children to build a wide range of things. Today's young children, sitting at the computer, too often must learn to follow the sometimes quite inflexible trajectories that designers have programmed for them and, despite all of the talk of choice, may live in a much more structured world than their parents did when they were children.

# REFERENCES

Aristotle (2004) *The History of Animals*. Whitefish, MT: Kessinger Publications.

Barthes, R. (1967). *Elements of Semiology*. New York: Hill and Wang.

———(1973). *Mythologies*. London: Paladin.

———(1977). *Image-Music-Text*. London: Fontana.

Bell, A. (1985). "One Rule of News English: Geographical, Social and Historical Spread." *Te Reo* 28:95–117.

Berger, J. (1972). *Ways of Seeing*. Harmondsworth, England: Penguin.

Berger, P. L. (1966). *Invitation to Sociology*. Harmondsworth, England: Penguin.

Berger, P., and Luckmann, T. (1966). *The Social Construction of Reality*. Harmondsworth, England: Penguin.

Bergson, H. (1966). *Durée et Simultanéité*. Paris: Presses Universitaires de France.

Bernstein, B. (1971). *Class, Codes and Control*, Vol. 1. *Theoretical Studies towards a Sociology of Language*. London: Routledge.

———(1981). "Codes, Modalities and the Process of Cultural Reproduction: A Model." *Language and Society* 19:327–63.

———(1986). "On Pedagogic Discourse." In J. Richardson (Ed.), *Handbook for Theory and Research in the Sociology of Education* (pp. 205–90). Westport, CT: Greenwood.

———(1990). *The Structuring of Pedagogic Discourse*. London: Routledge.

Bettelheim, B. (1979). *The Uses of Enchantment*. Harmondsworth, England: Penguin.

Boje, A. (1971). *Open Plan Offices*. London: Business Books.

Bols, P., Houppermans, M., Krijger, C., Lentjes, W., Savelkouls, T., Terlingen, M., and Teune, P. (1986). *Werk aan de Wereld*. Den Bosch, Netherlands: Malmberg.

Bourdieu, P. (1977). *Outline of a Theory of Practice*. Cambridge: Cambridge University Press.

———(1986). *Distinction: A Social Critique of the Judgment of Taste*. Cambridge: Polity.

Brown, G., and Yule, G. (1987). *Discourse Analysis*. Cambridge: Cambridge University Press.

Caldas-Coulthard, C. R., and Van Leeuwen, T. (2002). "Stunning, Shimmering, Iridescent: Toys as the Representation of Gendered Social Actors." In J. Sunderland and L. Litosseliti (Eds.), *Gender Identity and Discourse Analysis* (pp. 91–108). Amsterdam, Netherlands: Benjamins.

————(2003). "Teddy Bear Stories." *Social Semiotics* 13(1):5–29.

Cassidy, C. (1965). *We Like Kindergarten*. New York: Golden.

Chernoff, J. M. (1979). *African Rhythm and African Sensibility: Aesthetics and Social Action in African Musical Idioms*. Chicago: University of Chicago Press.

Cleave, C., Jowett, S., and Bate, M. (1982). *And So to School: A Study of Continuity from Pre-School to Infant School*. London: NFER-Nelson.

Curthoys, A., and Docker, J. (1989). "In Praise of Prisoner." In J. Tulloch and G. Turner (Eds.), *Australian Television: Programs, Pleasures and Politics* (pp. 39–51). Sydney: Allen and Unwin.

Davies, G., and Omer, O. (1966). "Time Allocation and Marketing." *Time and Society* 5(2):253–68.

Davis, M. (1990). *Miles: The Autobiography*. London: Macmillan.

Durkheim, E. (1976). *The Elementary Forms of Religious Life*. London: Allen and Unwin.

Durkheim, E., and Mauss, M. (1963). *Primitive Classification*. London: Cohen and West.

Eley, J., and Marmot, A. F. (1995). *Understanding Offices: What Every Manager Needs to Know about Offices*. London: Penguin.

Elias, N. (1992). *Time: An Essay*. Oxford: Blackwell.

Evans-Pritchard, E. E. (1940). *The Nuer*. Oxford: Oxford University Press.

Fairclough, N. (1989a). *Language and Power*. London: Longman.

————(1989b). "Critical and Descriptive Goals in Discourse Analysis." *Journal of Pragmatics* 9:739–63.

————(1992). *Discourse and Social Change*. Cambridge: Polity.

Foucault, M. (1977). *Language, Counter-Memory, Practice*, ed. D. F. Bouchard and S. Simon. Ithaca, NY: Cornell University Press.

————(1978). *The History of Sexuality*, Vol. 1. Harmondsworth, England: Penguin.

————(1979). *Discipline and Punish: The Birth of the Prison*. Harmondsworth, England: Penguin.

Fowler, R. (1991). *Language in the News: Discourse and Ideology in the Press*. London: Routledge.

Fowler, R., Hodge, R., Kress, G., and Trew, T. (1979). *Language and Control*. London: Routledge.

Freud, S. (1975 [1901]). *The Psychopathology of Everyday Life*. Harmondsworth, England: Penguin.

Gleason, H. A., Jr. (1973). "Contrastive Analysis in Discourse Structure." In A. Makkai and D. G. Lockwood (Eds.), *Readings in Stratificational Linguistics* (pp. 258–76). Tuscaloosa: University of Alabama Press.

Glen, M. (1997). "Ruby." In S. Gretz (Ed.), *The Hutchinson Treasury of Teddy Bear Tales* (pp. 24–34). London: Hutchinson.

Goffman, E. (1959). *The Presentation of Self in Everyday Life*. Harmondsworth, England: Penguin.

————(1974). "On Face-Work: An Analysis of Ritual Elements in Social Interaction." In B. G. Blount (Ed.), *Language, Culture, and Society* (pp. 224–50). Cambridge, MA: Winthrop.

Grimes, J. (1977). *The Thread of Discourse*. The Hague: Mouton.

Grossin, W. (1990). "Les représentations culturelles de temps comme condition de l'histoire." *Technologies, Idéologies, Pratiques* 8(1–4):297–312.

Habermas, J. (1976). *Legitimation Crisis*. London: Heinemann.

————(1984). *The Theory of Communicative Action*, Vol. 1. *Reason and the Rationalization of Society*. Boston: Beacon.

Hall, S. (1982). "The Determination of News Photographs." In S. Cohen and J. Young (Eds.), *The Manufacture of News* (pp. 226–43). London: Constable.

Halliday, M. A. K. (1967–1968). "Notes on Transitivity and Theme in English," parts 1, 2, and 3. *Journal of Linguistics* 3(1):37–81; 3(2):199–244; 4(2):179–215.

———(1973). *Explorations in the Functions of Language*. London: Longman.

———(1975). *Learning How to Mean*. London: Arnold.

———(1978). *Language as Social Semiotic*. London: Arnold.

———(1985). *An Introduction to Functional Grammar*. London: Arnold.

Halliday, M. A. K., and Hasan, R. (1976). *Cohesion in English*. London: Longman.

Hermeren, G. (1969). *Representation and Meaning in the Visual Arts*. Lund, Sweden: Scandinavian University Books.

Hodge, B., and Kress, G. (1988). *Social Semiotics*. Cambridge: Polity.

Holt, J. (1970). *The Underachieving School*. Harmondsworth, England: Penguin.

Iedema, R. (2000). "Bureaucratic Planning and Resemiotisation." In E. Ventola (Ed.), *Discourse and Community* (pp. 47–70). Tübingen: Gunter Narr Verlag.

Illich, I. (1973). *Deschooling Society*. Harmondsworth, England: Penguin.

———(1976). *Disabling Professions*. London: Marion Boyars.

Jones, C. (1989). *The Search for Meaning*, Vol. 2. Sydney: ABC Publications.

Kirschner, S. (2003). "Time, Power and Law: The Legitimation of the War on Iraq and the Timing of the Search for Weapons of Mass Destruction. A Critical Discourse Analysis." Unpublished M.A. dissertation, Cardiff University.

Kress, G. (1983). "Linguistic and Ideological Transformations in News Reporting." In H. Davis and P. Walton (Eds.), *Language, Image, Media* (pp. 120–39). Oxford: Blackwell.

———(1985a). *Linguistic Processes in Sociocultural Practice*. Geelong, Australia: Deakin University Press.

———(1985b). "Discourses, Texts, Readers and the Pro-Nuclear Arguments." In P. Chilton (Ed.), *Language and the Nuclear Arms Debate: Nukespeak Today* (pp. 141–76). London: Frances Pinter.

Kress, G., and Hodge, R. (1979). *Language as Ideology*. London: Routledge.

Kress, G., Jewitt, C., Bourne, J., Franks, A., Hardcastle, J., Jones, K., and Reid, E. (2005). *English in Urban Classrooms*. London: Routledge.

Kress, G., and Threadgold, T. (1988). "Towards a Social Theory of Genre." *Southern Review* 21(3):215–43.

Kress, G., and Van Leeuwen, T. (1990). *Reading Images*. Geelong, Australia: Deakin University Press.

Kress, G. and Van Leeuwen, T. (2007). *Reading Images—The Grammar of Visual Design*. Second Edition. London: Routledge.

Labov, W. (1972). "The Transformation of Experience in Narrative Syntax." In W. Labov, *Language in the Inner City* (pp. 354–96). Philadelphia: University of Philadelphia Press.

Lakoff, G., and Johnson, M. (1980). *Metaphors We Live By*. Chicago: University of Chicago Press.

Leech, G. (1966). *English in Advertising*. London: Longman.

Leete-Hodge, E. (n.d.). *Mark and Mandy*. London: Peter Haddock.

Lemke, J. (1983). "Thematic Analysis: Systems, Structures and Strategies." *Recherches Sémiotiques/Semiotic Inquiry* 3(2):159–87.

———(1985). *Using Language in the Classroom*. Geelong, Australia: Deakin University Press.

———(1987a). "Textual Politics: Heteroglossia, Discourse Analysis, and Social Dynamics." Unpublished paper, Department of Education, City University of New York.

———(1987b). "Technical Discourse and Technocratic Ideology." Paper presented at the Eighth AILA Congress (Association Internationale de Linguistique Appliquée), University of Sydney, 16–21 August.

Levinson, S. C. (1983). *Pragmatics*. Cambridge: Cambridge University Press.

Lévi-Strauss, C. (1964). *Totemism*. Harmondsworth, England: Penguin.

———(1967). "The Story of Asdiwal." In E. Leach (Ed.), *The Structural Study of Myth and Totemism* (pp. 49–69). London: Tavistock.

Luck, M. (1990). *Your Child and Success at School*. Sydney: Murdoch Books.

Machin, D., and Van Leeuwen, T. (2003). "Global Schemas and Local Discourses in *Cosmopolitan*." *Journal of Sociolinguistics* 7(4):493–513.

———(2004). "Global Media: Generic Homogeneity and Discursive Diversity." *Continuum* 18(1):99–120.

Malinowski, B. (1923). "The 'Problem of Meaning in Primitive Languages." In C. K. Ogden and I. A. Richards (Eds.), *The Meaning of Meaning* (pp. 296–336). London: Routledge and Kegan Paul.

———(1935). *Coral Gardens and Their Magic*, Vol. 2. London: Allen and Unwin.

Mansell, D. (1991). *My Old Teddy*. London: Walker.

Martin, J. R. (1984a). "Lexical Cohesion, Field and Genre: Parceling Experience and Discourse Goals." In J. E. Copeland (Ed.), *Linguistics and Semiotics: Text Semantics and Discourse Semantics: Proceedings of the Second Rice Symposium* (pp. 297–306). Houston, TX: Rice University Press.

———(1984b). "Language, Register and Genre." In F. Christie (Ed.), *Language Studies: Children Writing* (pp. 21–30). Geelong, Australia: Deakin University Press.

———(1985). *Factual Writing: Exploring and Challenging Social Reality*. Geelong, Australia: Deakin University Press.

———(1988). "Literacy in Science: Learning to Handle Text on Technology." In F. Christie (Ed.), *A Fresh Look at the Basics: The Concept of Literacy* (pp. 79–117). Hawthorn, Victoria: Australian Council for Educational Research.

———(1989). "Technicality and Abstraction: Language for the Creation of Specialised Texts." In F. Christie (Ed.), *Writing in Schools: Reader* (pp. 36–44). Geelong, Australia: Deakin University Press.

———(1992). *English Text: System and Structure*. Amsterdam, Netherlands: Benjamins.

———(2000). "Beyond Exchange: APPRAISAL Systems in English." In S. Hunston and G. Thompson (Eds.), *Evaluation in Text* (pp. 142–72). Oxford: Oxford University Press.

Martin, J. R., Wignell, P., Eggins, C., and Rothery, J. (1988). "Secret English: Discourse Technology in a Junior Secondary School." In L. Gerot, J. Oldenburg, and T. Van Leeuwen (Eds.), *Language and Socialisation: Home and School: Proceedings from the Working Conference of Language in Education*. Sydney: Macquarie University.

Matthiessen, C. (1992). *Lexicogrammatical Cartography: English Systems*. Sydney: Department of Linguistics, University of Sydney.

Mead, G. H. (1934). *Mind, Self and Society*. Chicago: Chicago University Press.

Morgan, H. (1985). *Mary Kate and the School Bus*. London: Puffin.

Moyo, J. G. (1976). *Beginning to Learn*. London: Longman.

Mumford, L. (1934). *Technics and Civilization*. New York: Harcourt, Brace.

Nederveen Pieterse, J. (1992). *White on Black: Images of Africa and Blacks in Western Popular Culture*. New Haven, CT: Yale University Press.

Negt, O. (1984). *Lebendige Arbeit, enteignete Zeit*. Frankfurt: Campus Verlag.

Nowotny, O. (1984). *Eigenzeit: Entstehung und Strukturierung eines Zeitgefühls*. Frankfurt: Suhrkamp.

Oakley, M. (1985). *Our Society and Others*. Sydney: McGraw-Hill.

O'Halloran, K. (2005). *Mathematical Discourse: Language, Symbolism and Visual Images*. London: Continuum.

Paolucci, G. (1996). "The Changing Dynamics of Working Time." *Time and Society* 5(2):145–67.

Parsons, T. (1977). *The Structure of Social Action*. Chicago: Free Press.

Pearce, P. (1986). "Lion at School." In S. Corrin and S. Corrin (Eds.), *Stories for Five-Year-Olds*. Harmondsworth, England: Penguin.

Propp, V. (1968 [1927]). *Morphology of the Folktale*. Austin: University of Texas Press.

Quirk, R., Greenbaum, S., Leech, G., and Svartvik, J. (1972). *A Grammar of Contemporary English*. London: Longman.

Renwick, M. (1987). *Going to School: A Guide for Parents*. Wellington: New Zealand Ministry of Education.

Schank, R., and Abelson, R. (1977). *Scripts, Plans, Goals and Understanding*. Hillsdale, NJ: Erlbaum.

Simenon, G. (1979). *Maigret and the Spinster*. Harmondsworth, England: Penguin.

Sontag, S. (1979). *Illness as Metaphor*. London: Allen Lane.

*Starting School Coloring Book*. (1981). Deerfield, IL: Channing L. Bete.

Thompson, E. P. (1967). "Time, Work-Discipline and Industrial Capitalism." *Past and Present* 38:56–97.

Toffler, A. (1970). *Futureshock*. London: Bodley Head.

Trew, T. (1979). "Theory and Ideology at Work." In R. Fowler, R. Hodge, G. Kress, and T. Trew (Eds.), *Language and Control* (pp. 94–116). London: Routledge.

Tuchman, G., Kaplan Daniels, A., and Benet, J. (1978). *Hearth and Home: Images of Women in the Mass Media*. New York: Oxford University Press.

Van Dijk, T. A. (1991). *Racism in the Press*. London: Routledge.

———(1993). *Elite Discourse and Racism*. London: Sage.

Van Leeuwen, J. (1981). *De Metro van Magnus*. The Hague: Omniboek.

Van Leeuwen, T. (1987a). "Generic strategies in Press Journalism." *Australian Review of Applied Linguistics* 10(2):199–220.

———(1987b). "Music and Ideology: Notes towards a Sociosemiotics of Mass Media Music." Sydney Association for the Study of Society and Culture. *SASSC Working Papers* 2(1–2):19–45.

———(1993a). "Genre and Field in Critical Discourse Analysis: A Synopsis." *Discourse and Society* 4(2):193–225.

———(1993b). "Language and Representation: The Recontextualisation of Participants, Activities and Reactions." Unpublished Ph.D. thesis, University of Sydney.

———(1995). "Representing Social Action," *Discourse and Society* 6(1):81–106.

———(1996). "The Representation of Social Actors." In C. R. Caldas-Coulthard and M. Coulthard (Eds.), *Texts and Practices: Readings in Critical Discourse Analysis* (pp. 32–70). London: Routledge.

———(1999). *Speech, Music, Sound*. London: Macmillan.

———(2000a). "The Construction of Purpose in Discourse." In S. Sarangi and M. Coulthard (Eds.), *Discourse and Social Life* (pp. 66–82). London: Longman.

———(2000b). "Visual Racism." In M. Reisigl and R. Wodak (Eds.), *The Semiotics of Racism: Approaches in Critical Discourse Analysis* (pp. 330–50). Vienna: Passagen Verlag.

———(2005a). *Introducing Social Semiotics*. London: Routledge.

———(2005b). "Time in Discourse." *Linguistics and the Human Sciences* 1(1):125–45.

———(2007). "Legitimation in Discourse and Communication." *Discourse and Communication* 1(1): 91–112.

Van Leeuwen, T., and Caldas-Coulthard, C. R. (2004). "The Semiotics of Kinetic Design." In D. Banks (Ed.), *Text and Texture: Systemic-Functional Viewpoints on the Nature and Structure of Text* (pp. 355–80). Paris: L'Harmattan.

Van Leeuwen, T., and Wodak, R. (1999). "Legitimizing Immigration Control: A Discourse-Historical Analysis." *Discourse Studies* 1(1):83–119.

Von Sturmer, J. (1981). "Talking with Aborigines." *Australian Institute of Aboriginal Studies Newsletter* 15:13–30.

Weber, M. (1977). *The Theory of Social and Economic Organization*. New York: Free Press.

Whorf, B. L. (1956). *Language, Thought and Reality*, Cambridge, MA: MIT Press.

Winnicott, D. W. (1971). *Playing and Reality*. London: Tavistock.

Wright, W. (1975). *Sixguns and Society: A Structural Study of the Western*. Berkeley and Los Angeles: University of California Press.

Zijderveld, A. C. (1979). *On Clichés: The Supersedure of Meaning by Function in Modernity*. London: Routledge.

# INDEX

LaVergne, TN USA
11 January 2011
211821LV00001B/1/P